MW00398443

SUN SIGN
KARMA

© Keith Papke

About the Author

Bernie Ashman is a highly respected professional astrologer who has been studying, practicing, and teaching for over thirty-five years. He is the author of several books and has contributed to the astrology magazines *Dell Horoscope, Astro Signs, The Mountain Astrologer,* and *Welcome to Planet Earth*. Bernie also gives personal readings, conducts lectures, and contributes to astrology software programs. His Past Life software program is based on a chart he invented and is being sold internationally by Cosmic Patterns in Gainesville, Florida. Visit www.astrologysoftware.com/pro/win_writer /past_lives.html to learn more about the program. Bernie lives in Durham, North Carolina.

SUN SIGN
KARMA

Resolving Past Life Patterns with Astrology

BERNIE ASHMAN

Llewellyn Publications
Woodbury, Minnesota

Sun Sign Karma: Resolving Past Life Patterns with Astrology © 2021 by Bernie Ashman. All rights reserved. No part of this book may be used or reproduced in any manner whatsoever, including internet usage, without written permission from Llewellyn Publications, except in the case of brief quotations embodied in critical articles and reviews.

First Edition
First Printing, 2021

Book design by Samantha Peterson
Cover design by Kevin R. Brown

Llewellyn Publications is a registered trademark of Llewellyn Worldwide Ltd.

Library of Congress Cataloging-in-Publication Data
Names: Ashman, Bernie, author.
Title: Sun sign karma : resolving past life patterns with astrology /
 Bernie Ashman.
Description: First edition. | Woodbury, Minnesota : Llewellyn Publications,
 2021. | Summary: "Catalogs the strengths, challenges, common karmic
 shadows, and keys to making positive changes for each astrological
 sign"— Provided by publisher.
Identifiers: LCCN 2021007316 (print) | LCCN 2021007317 (ebook) | ISBN
 9780738766911 (paperback) | ISBN 9780738767024 (ebook)
Subjects: LCSH: Astrology and reincarnation. | Zodiac. | Karma.
Classification: LCC BF1729.R37 A82 2021 (print) | LCC BF1729.R37 (ebook)
 | DDC 133.5—dc23
LC record available at https://lccn.loc.gov/2021007316
LC ebook record available at https://lccn.loc.gov/2021007317

Llewellyn Worldwide Ltd. does not participate in, endorse, or have any authority or responsibility concerning private business transactions between our authors and the public.

All mail addressed to the author is forwarded but the publisher cannot, unless specifically instructed by the author, give out an address or phone number.

Any internet references contained in this work are current at publication time, but the publisher cannot guarantee that a specific location will continue to be maintained. Please refer to the publisher's website for links to authors' websites and other sources.

Llewellyn Publications
A Division of Llewellyn Worldwide Ltd.
2143 Wooddale Drive
Woodbury, MN 55125-2989
www.llewellyn.com

Printed in the United States of America

Also by Bernie Ashman

Astrological Games People Play

How to Survive Mercury Retrograde

Intuition and Your Sun Sign

Roadmap to Your Future

SignMates

Sun Signs & Past Lives

CONTENTS

INTRODUCTION

This is a book that in many ways will guide you to more readily integrate past-life karmic relationship energies into the current life. Each of us comes into this life with memories from past lives, many of them hidden on an unconscious level. As we proceed on our journey, various life encounters activate these memories. It is true that we can make use of past-life talents. We may have a past-life memory bank full of positive skills we learned in past lives that can be tapped into, aiding us in maintaining balanced relationships in this incarnation. There are some past-life themes that can impede our growth and paths to greater fulfillment. A major focus of this book is to identify those past-life-relating patterns that correspond to each astrological sign. These energies don't have to play a big role in our lives. The sign chapters in this book offer the keys to a road map that will unlock the paths to go beyond the pull of past-life patterns.

In my experience as an astrologer, it is a misconception to think of the astrological Sun sign that you were born into as giving you traits only developed in this life. There is an excellent chance you have past-life instincts that have carried over into this lifetime.

It is the karmic patterns that find us repeating behaviors that keep us stuck in limiting situations that we need to channel into more productive expressions. I think of these karmic patterns as energies that reside in the shadow part of our consciousness that need to be brought out into clearer light. Each of us has some of these karmic shadows following us into this life. Think of this as unfinished business for this incarnation that we can learn to master. Much of my astrological counseling over the years has been helping people navigate through karmic patterns. Many of these karmic tendencies are linked to past-life relationships. What is interesting is that some people don't know a karmic pattern was supposed to be already over in this life. Why do we keep repeating old, worn-out past-life behaviors? There can be an attachment to these shadowy influences because we get used to acting them out. It is as though they know our name and feel free to come calling. They can take on a life of their own. We do have the freedom to opt out of negative thoughts and actions. But it can take acknowledging these shadow energies exist in us. It is at this time we can begin to find the inner strength and clarity to walk away from karmic patterns. It might take some willpower and positive reinforcement, but we can divorce ourselves from these past patterns of thinking.

Karmic Pattern Recognition

Even in the best relationships a karmic pattern can show its face and try to weave its way into your thinking. A relationship might not be a karmic one but can still stir up past-life tendencies. Don't panic. Sometimes it is in an emotional or angry reaction that each of us can fall victim to past-life behaviors. Our mind might be telling us we are acting out a learned behavior from this lifetime. There is an excellent chance the behavior and thoughts are carryovers from previous lifetimes. With some practice, you will get better at catching these past-life impulses. What is the payoff for doing this? You will feel empowered, and your relationships with lovers, friends, family, and businesspeople will grow clearer and stronger.

Past-life patterns from previous incarnations can still be with us in the current incarnation. They are in our memory bank and can get activated in this lifetime. They can reside out of the awareness of our conscious mind on a subconscious level. The key thing to remember is that you can find a positive way to make use of this energy. The reward is enjoying greater harmony and fulfillment in your relationships.

How Does Your Current-Life Sun Sign Link with Your Past Incarnations?

In reading the past-life patterns in the sign chapters that correspond to your Sun sign, you will soon realize that there is another dimension contained within your sign. Your Sun sign is the portal through which you can identify past-life patterns. This is not saying you have always incarnated with the same Sun sign. Think of it as becoming more aware of the past-life patterns you have come into this life to gain clarity about through the Sun sign you have from birth. This Sun sign is only specific to this lifetime so you can get a better handle on past-life patterns from previous incarnations that you came here to better express productively. Your Sun sign is not causing these past-life patterns to occur again, but rather it is a vehicle through which to identify and heal these past-life patterns and bring yourself happier and balanced relationships. The powerful radiance of your own Sun sign can guide you to find the insight to find an alternative expression to heal a past-life pattern.

The Twelve Astrological Signs: Ambassadors of Transformation

The sign of the zodiac on the day of birth is known as our Sun sign, and it gives each of us unique personalities. Each sign guides us in its own way to make choices that steer us away from karmic patterns that can interfere with our personal road to fulfillment. There is the light of transformation in the framework of each of the astrological signs.

If you were born into the fire sign Aries tribe, you possess a natural expression for displaying fast actions and often can be a risk-taker. Patience and focus come as you gain greater insight into your most important goals. When you channel your inner restlessness productively, life is a happier experience. Your trailblazing spirit can give you the inner strength to stare down any karmic pattern obstruction in your path.

If you were born into the earth sign Taurus tribe, you are attracted to life experiences that have a stabilizing effect. You likely have a tendency to move carefully with a sense of purpose. You resist change if it is not on your own terms. Your way of staying focused empowers you with a rugged determination to push through any karmic pattern.

If you were born into the air sign Gemini tribe, the universe has given you immense communication power accompanied by a strong mental nature. You are at your best when having multiple life paths to pursue. Your curiosity about a wide variety of subjects keeps your mind stimulated. Your ability to decipher ways to integrate karmic patterns into your life makes for a happier journey.

If you were born into the water sign Cancer tribe, you likely operate with a deep emotional nature. You have a tendency to move cautiously but with an underlying strategy to achieve goals. Finding the right home is highly valued. You are probably very particular about which people you will allow to get close to you. Your powerful intuition can guide you to successfully navigate through karmic patterns.

If you were born into the fire sign Leo tribe, you have a lionlike dramatic self-expression. Your charismatic personality can make you the center of attention. An ability to convince others of your ideas is what often leads to making your dreams come true. It is your willpower that gives you the opportunity to work your way through karmic patterns.

If you were born into the earth sign Virgo tribe, you are gifted with learning skills that bring you new opportunities. People likely perceive you as being analytical and hardworking. Realizing that perfection can be the enemy of the good keeps you happier. It is your tenacity at problem-solving that helps you figure out how to rise above karmic patterns.

If you were born into the air sign Libra tribe, you are likely partnership-oriented. It is not that you can't be independent but more that you desire to share your life with others. A mental and emotional balance is highly valued. You get clear vision of the past, present, and future when you take the time to recharge your mental batteries. Your drive to seek a sense of inner peace is often the motivation to conquer karmic patterns.

If you were born into the water sign Scorpio tribe, you have a natural tendency to express yourself with deep emotions and passion. Your loyalty to people wins their love and friendship. When you are able to trust your intuition, life seems more user friendly. Your survival instincts are strong, allowing you to overcome obstacles in the path of your goals. It is your determination to experience a true sense of personal power that allows you to not let karmic patterns keep you from finding authentic happiness and fulfillment.

If you were born into the fire sign Sagittarius tribe, you were given an inspiring spirit that thrives on seeking adventure. It is your optimism that is the road to new opportunity. People probably perceive you as lucky, and you might wonder why others don't have such good fortune as often as you do. When you develop a broad life philosophy, the universe rewards you with new stimulating experiences. It is your never-ending positive thinking that prepares you to successfully turn karmic patterns into energies of hope for a brighter today and tomorrow.

If you were born into the earth sign Capricorn tribe, chances are you have a serious demeanor with a strong focusing ability. Ambition colors your thoughts. You have a tendency to be serious about commitments. Your follow-through on a job has no sign rival. You attract responsibility, so you do need to be careful about how much work you accept. You like people you can count on when you need support. Your inner strength magnifies when you trust your ability to succeed. It is your determination to face the reality of karmic patterns when they arise that truly empowers you.

If you were born into the air sign Aquarius tribe, you are an individualist with unique insights. You likely live for the future as the present does sometimes bore you. Your mind tends to enjoy people with new ideas. You probably have a wide variety of friends. Romantic partners are likely friends as well as lovers. Some people see you as aloof, but you like to think of this as remaining objective. Your mental side probably outweighs your emotional expression. It is your unique way to see outside of the box that guides you to learn from karmic pattern energy and put it to creative use.

If you were born into the water sign Pisces tribe, you have a vivid, dreamy imagination that is moved to act on ideals. Some people could perceive you as passive, but you view this as your way of processing your thoughts. You are a romantic with strong feelings. Your inner being can be a poet and artist. Reality is not always what drives you toward success. You are more likely following an inwardly inspired path. You can fall in love with the ideals of a lover. It is your willingness to learn from the past that allows you to treat karmic patterns as teachers gifting you new wisdom.

Each sign has a unique way to inspire us to rise above karmic shadows. Sometimes the lighted path to a sense of rebirth is closer than you think. You will read in the sign chapters the keys to rising above karmic challenges.

In acupuncture and massage there are pressure points in our body that can be worked on to release bottled-up energies causing discomfort. In a similar way our signs can be tuned and used as a way to release us from the hold of karmic patterns. Each sign contains a magical formula to guide you to let go of shadowy karmic baggage that will lighten your load as you walk your journey through life and find greater relationship fulfillment.

Don't ever underestimate the transformative power of each astrological sign. The universe works in magical ways through your own sign and the other eleven. Any karmic pattern corresponding to an astrological sign in this book can be lifted out of a negative hold from past incarnations into the radiant light with a refreshed clarity in this life.

Forgiveness: A Powerful Ally

Forgiveness can be the lubricant to allow you to turn a karmic pattern into a winner. Sometimes it is the leftover memories of past-life relationships that did not go well that gives a karmic pattern life in this incarnation. As you read your own sign chapter, you may become aware that you are repeating a past-life karmic pattern in the current life. If you can forgive someone in this life, you might be releasing the hold a past-life pattern has on you and creating a revitalized ability to enjoy greater relationship happiness in the current incarnation. Reading your own sign chapter will show you how to neutralize a past-life pattern's energy.

It could be you need to forgive yourself. Sometimes we hold on to too much guilt resulting from our relationships. Forgiveness is a potential opportunity to send a karmic pattern away from you. Following the forgiveness footsteps is an empowering way to let go of the past. Often it will heal karmic tendencies in relating to others.

Helpful Hints before Reading the Sign Chapters

Try to remember nobody is perfect as you read about possible past-life karmic relationship patterns associated with your own astrological sign that could occur. We each came into this life with lessons to learn. Relationships usually stir up our emotions more than any other area of life. Romantic relationships can often awaken a past-life tendency that you will identify in your sign chapter. It can be that in recognizing a past-life pattern, your insights will become empowered. Think of this book as a guide to creating more balanced relationships with all the main people in your life. When we gain clarity about past-life impulses and patterns that influence our mind, a transformation can occur. We can enjoy a greater sense of fulfillment brightening the skies of our present and future!

ONE
ARIES: THE WARRIOR

Dates: March 21 to April 19

Element: Fire

Strengths: Courage, fighting spirit, adventurous

Challenges: Impatience, impulsiveness, lack of focus

Karmic Relationship Primary Shadow: Fear of learning from the past

Key to Transforming Karmic Patterns: Facing adversity

The Aries Current-Life Relationship Landscape

If you were born under the sign of Aries, you need a vast territory from which to operate. You possess a restless spirit that enjoys being challenged. Your competitive nature offers you an endless amount of energy to reach your goals. You appreciate your talents being recognized. The traditional astrology mantra for your sign is "I am."

Your identity is important to you in that a strong sense of self propels you into action. People able to notice your abilities draw you closer.

You likely enjoy people with lively personalities. You prefer individuals to get to the point quickly in communicating their expectations of you. Entering relationships quickly is a trait of your sign.

You might be more sensitive than people realize until they get to know you. Your emotional nature can be covered with an external persona of strength so much of the time that outside observers don't detect a strong feeling part of you.

Learning patience with others brings them closer. You prefer people who respect your need for freedom. A lover or friend able to understand your spontaneous ideas excites you.

Your identity is a special connection to your spirit. In many ways it is a sacred part of you, whether you reveal this openly to others or keep it hidden until you trust someone. People who empower you become close allies. They have a special way of elevating your self-confidence. These people discover the key to the portal that opens to your heart and the fountain of your love.

The Aries Past-Life Karmic Relationship Patterns

Each of us has brought past-life memory patterns into this lifetime with us. You likely will not find that each of the following karmic relationship patterns being discussed is a regular part of your own experience. Pay special attention to the ones that seem like a piece of your current journey. Nothing written in this book is meant to pass judgment on you. Think of this as a path to personal empowerment. By acknowledging a past-life pattern, you are taking the first step to transforming the energy into an enlightening insight.

As an Aries, your boldness will inspire you to rise above karmic patterns that could be keeping you from fulfilling relationships. It can take much practice to overcome a karmic pattern. Don't get discouraged if you fall back into a behavior after you acknowledge its presence in your life. This is a typical occurrence for everyone. It is definitely a learning experience. The important thing is to keep trying to improve.

Lack of Assertion

There might have been incarnations in which you said yes too many times when you really wanted to say no. If this sounds familiar as a regular impulse in this life when interacting with others, then this is very possibly a repeating theme that followed you into this incarnation. It can easily throw your relationships out of balance. Due to this behavior, you are unable to establish the equality you desire in relationships. Your personal happiness is not where you want it to be if you are giving to the extreme. The give and take in your partnerships needs an adjustment.

This karmic pattern often attracts people to you who have controlling behaviors. Your own goals are not seen as important to a person extremely focused on their own dreams. It can feel like a real slap in the face if your own hopes and wishes are not valued. An Aries thrives on having their ideas encouraged by others. Your fiery spirit evaporates into steam if you become too trapped by this past-life theme.

Playing the Blame Game

This is a past-life pattern that can find you constantly blaming people for your problems, which takes away from your road to personal empowerment. Rather than getting caught up in regularly finding fault with others, you benefit more from paying attention to solutions to problems. This is not saying to feel too responsible for situations not going well. Your Aries mental strength is energized in a more productive way when you don't allow yourself to become ensnared by the entanglement of this karmic net. Your own goals get diluted if you put excess energy in holding others accountable for what they seem to be doing to interfere with your plans. Believing more in your own ability to fulfill your goals is far better than looking to accuse others of blocking your road to success.

Power Struggles

This pattern left over from past incarnations can sometimes be experienced in your relating to others like a tug-of-war. Your ideas can forcefully clash with people. Your negotiating tactics may be missing. There could have been past incarnations in which you did not believe in compromise. "Might makes right" was your mantra. If this pattern of behavior gets awakened in this lifetime, it tends to alienate those you want to remain close to. Creating win-win solutions remains out of reach if you lock horns endlessly with others. Much time gets wasted and you can end up very frustrated. The winning becomes too important and does not help you establish the victory formula for relationship success. The harmony you seek will remain beyond your reach when allowing this past-life shadow to cover your clearer perceptions.

Intense Adrenaline Rush

Your sign is known for moving fast. In past incarnations you could have had a tendency to move quickly into romantic relationships. If you have gotten into trouble by throwing caution to the wind, this might be an instinct still with you. Your assertiveness and fast pace can take you to new creative heights. There are times this same energy does not serve you as well in relationships. You could be too trusting of others at the beginning of relationships to the point of lacking clear judgment. Because you are an Aries, the universe does bless you with incredible energy. It is the excitement of meeting someone new that can fog your perceptions if you get in too big of a hurry. Another side of this pattern is changing directions so quickly that it confuses others. You might show a lack of consistency to the point that people will not know what to expect from you.

Hiding from the Truth

It could be that in some past incarnations you did not accept criticism very well. This was especially true when someone pointed out how you repeated certain behaviors no matter how many times you were told they were upsetting. If this karmic pattern is awakened in this lifetime, it can add great tension to your relationships with lovers, friends, family members, or work colleagues. If you have been repeating actions that irritate those closest to you without making any adjustments, you will alienate people. Denial only serves to enlarge problems. Refusing to listen or engage in clear communication creates distance with others. Your sense of fulfillment will eventually feel much lower than you desire.

Frozen Momentum

If this pattern followed you into this incarnation, you might leave love relationships too soon, not giving them a chance to develop. There are different reasons this might occur if the pattern gets awakened regularly. One is a fear of closeness. When someone wants to learn more about your emotional nature, it could be your signal to leave. You could be with someone who would be good for you, but your reluctance to invest enough time can be a problem. Another reason for an early exit is an inner restlessness. Giving a relationship enough time to turn into a solid commitment does not appeal to you. The idea that you might be missing out on meeting someone new is more exciting. This may constantly keep you from settling into a long-term relationship if you really want this to happen. Closeness can seem smothering if you truly don't want to reveal yourself to a partner.

Extreme Me Focus

This karmic pattern is colored with too much "I am"-ness. If you are in the habit of making use of this behavior, you will for sure lose sight of the goals of a partner. This actually can cause great tension with people from all walks of life. A loss of awareness in what people close to you need weakens your bond with them. The support you want for your own goals will be much less than you desire. Aries is a sign offering you an intense drive to pursue your own dreams. This self-driven enthusiasm can become so extreme that you can easily lose sight of what others might need from you. This pattern of behavior will cause a loved one to feel like you are not listening to their need for you to pay attention to them.

Space Invasion

If you don't give people enough room to be themselves, it might be due to the resurfacing of a karmic pattern. It will make others uncomfortable if you are constantly invading someone's need to make their own decisions. Compromise is easier to attain when you value the independence of others. Trust issues are sometimes what launches this past-life tendency and introduces it into the current incarnation. The more you move onto the turf boundaries of someone in an unsolicited way, the more likely you will be met with anger or some form of resistance. An inner insecurity could be at the root of this pattern launching itself into this life. This pattern or karmic shadow will create great distance between you and others. There is another possibility with this pattern. You were the person in past incarnations who had their space too invaded. This could have resulted from not defining your boundaries clearly. Your own goals became lost in the wind as they were swallowed by the demands of other people. You may have attracted strong-willed individuals who had a way of superimposing their own hopes and dreams over your own. If this rings a bell with you, then it is likely this past-life pattern has manifested again. It causes a lack of balance in your relationships.

Extreme Competitiveness

Being competitive comes with being an Aries. Having the fiery and highly energetic Mars as your ruling planet goes far in explaining your attraction to competition. If you always must win an argument in your social interactions, it could be due to a past-life pattern making an entrance into this life. The result could be pushing people away. Winning at all costs can cause you to lose valuable people in your life. Give and take as a philosophy is a wiser idea to promote relationship peace and harmony. There is nothing wrong with being a competitive person. It is that drive that can bring career success and push your momentum toward a goal with great enthusiasm. In your personal people-relating, it can even give you the self-confidence to meet new friends, business associates, and lovers. If this past-life pattern has resurfaced in the current life, you need to express a less feisty way of having to come out the winner. Toning down a winner-takes-all attitude promotes relationship harmony.

Sabotaging a Relationship

If you regularly try to find ways to end a relationship even if there are no problems, this could be due to a past-life karmic pattern. Sometimes this is caused by a fear of the relationship failing at some point in the future. It could be you don't have the self-confidence that you deserve a long-term successful relationship, or it could be possible you feel that you are missing out on a better partner by remaining in a current situation. You might be looking for a perfect partner, which does make for a problem, or you may be demanding perfection from yourself that is impossible to deliver. If you are purposely looking to sabotage a relationship, you will never really learn if you are with the right person. If you focus on negative outlooks for a relationship, the end result is not going to be fulfilling.

Misguided Anger

Anger is an emotion. There are times when anger is an appropriate response. If you find yourself exploding suddenly at friends, family, or loved ones on a regular basis, it is possible this is a past-life pattern that has planted itself in your memory bank. If you are holding on to anger for extended time periods, it can rush out unexpectedly when you least anticipate it. It could be a holdover from past incarnations that need to be overcome. If you feel that anger will help you get your own way in relationships, it can form a feeling of resentment from those people you need in your life. If you don't channel your anger productively, this is an energy working against you.

Promises Not Delivered

Fire signs like yourself tend to exaggerate your capabilities at times. It is possible that as a past-life tendency in some incarnations, you promised more than you could accomplish. This in itself is not a bad thing because it is that extra thrust of self-confidence that catapults you to do great things. But you can frustrate and anger people if you don't follow through on a regular basis with promises. There may be specific behaviors you have pledged to change but fail over and over to do so. It might be true that as a karmic pattern, you tend to attract individuals into your current life that are the ones not completing what they intend to do for you. You can feel as though you are not valued when people exhibit this behavior.

Altered Perceptions: Aries Paths to Transforming Karmic Relationship Patterns

It takes more energy to cling to a karmic pattern than to let it go. The relief when one of these past-life shadowy patterns is conquered is well worth the effort. In some ways you could feel like a relationship has had a rebirth. Your mind might experience a recharge. You likely will wonder why it took so long to dispense with the negative hold on you that was interfering with forming good harmony in your important relationships.

If you identify with any of the karmic patterns discussed, try not to worry. There is a portal to walk through that can help you find your way out of a pattern. Sometimes a karmic past-life pattern can make you feel like your mind is lost in a maze. You can be searching for the exit out of the pattern and feel lost. It is possible your conscious mind is not aware you are regularly engaging in a karmic pattern in your relating to others. Hopefully this book will bring great confidence in facing a pattern so you can explore how to escape from its grasp. Awakening to the reality of a karmic pattern is the first step along a new path to a more productive use of this energy.

Lack of Assertion

The lack of assertion past-life pattern can be overcome by practicing putting yourself at the front of the line. You need to place a higher value on your own needs. It will take some regular practice to accomplish this. Eventually you will feel more empowered to the level you need to reach. If at first it feels awkward to be more assertive, don't worry. It is a common experience to take two steps forward and one step back with this past-life pattern. If you are often in the company of people with strong personalities, it could take a few tries to speak up more forcefully to have your voice heard. As an Aries, you came into this life to definitely have an equal seat at the table. There might be a person you need to drop as a friend or at least make it known their way of treating you is no longer acceptable. Sometimes getting out of the line of fire of people not looking out for your best interest is one of the paths to seeing your way out of this pattern.

Playing the Blame Game

You can rise above the negative pull in the playing the blame game pattern by accepting responsibility for your own actions. It often takes two people to contribute to a problem, but, then again, it requires the cooperation of both individuals to right the course. You will find your relationships with others have less tension when you are willing to work toward more productive results. Casting blame is usually a defense mechanism to hide that you are the cause of a problem in your relating to others. If you want to receive more support for your own goals, a good way to do this is to let go of a tendency to accuse others of being the source of your difficulties in life. You will experience much more fulfillment in your relationships when you make a serious commitment to release this karmic pattern.

Power Struggles

In the power struggles past-life pattern it comes down to knowing how to use that powerful Aries inner strength. The key here is to not make people feel like you are purposely trying to steamroll your ideas over their own without giving them a fair shot. It will take some practice in realizing when to push hard for your own ideas and when to pause and carefully consider options being presented to you. Getting your own way at all costs will put others on the defensive. Learning to listen and slow down your mind puts you on the road to great relationship harmony. People are more apt to admire you if you meet them halfway when you pitch them a plan. You will find it easier to attract love, intimacy, and emotional support through showing humility alongside power.

Intense Adrenaline Rush

If the intense adrenaline rush karmic pattern is still in your memory bank from past lives and has become active in your current life, it can be brought under control. How might you accomplish this? Slowing down before getting too involved in a relationship is one way to do this. Taking the time to get to know someone before leaping too fast into a relationship can open your eyes more clearly to whether or not you want to make a commitment. Also, including a partner or significant other in important decisions is vital to maintaining a successful relationship. Aries loves spontaneity. But constantly making snap decisions can disrupt the harmony in a relationship. If you keep others in the loop about your plans, you will find people more supportive of your goals.

Hiding from the Truth

Hiding from the truth is a karmic pattern that has its roots in denial. Nobody in reality is that happy about having their actions criticized. But acting like there is not a problem when there is one usually makes the problem bigger. However, sometimes it only takes displaying you are making an attempt to change a behavior to show you are listening. This is a good first step to alleviating the stress in a relationship. It is amazing how honest communication makes this past-life pattern evaporate as though it never existed. You will notice people respond positively when you show a commitment to surrendering behaviors that only serve to alienate others. When you stop trying to hide from the truth, a feeling of liberation takes its place.

Frozen Momentum

This prevents you from enjoying rubbing against the warm feet of a potentially fulfilling partner. Time together with a lover is essential to knowing the real depth of a relationship. If you stay longer in a relationship and truly explore the potential deeper love with someone, it could turn out to be a pleasant surprise. A relationship needs time to reveal its deeper rewards. Over time as you trust the commitment, the bond between you and another person grows in trust and strength. This is a past-life karmic pattern that will lessen its hold on your mind when you learn to appreciate the loving support that closeness with a person can deliver. It comes down to valuing the intimacy more than giving into running away. The roots of a relationship grow quickly when you stick around to enjoy the progressive growth of being with someone.

Extreme Me Focus

The extreme me focus past-life pattern can be overcome by facing the fact you are not paying equal attention to the important individuals in your life. It takes some time to turn a large ship around, and likewise you will need some effort to conquer this karmic pattern. If you accept the need to become a better listener, you will soon realize you are at least halfway beyond the grip of this pattern. Aries is a self-driven sign. The same strength you acquired at birth from this bold fire sign only needs to be focused on being more attentive to others. This does not require you to sacrifice your own goals. If you put in the determination to align your vision of today and tomorrow with that of another person, each of you benefits from the meeting of the minds.

Space Invasion

The space invasion past-life pattern can be alleviated by making sure you give others plenty of breathing room to feel free to exert their own version of independence. Sometimes this behavior is caused by feelings of inner insecurity. This can cause you not to trust people. You will find intimacy easier to establish when showing you trust someone. Relinquishing a need to control someone sets a relationship free to bring you much more fulfillment. The happiness you seek resides in giving a partner plenty of room to explore their own goals. It is then you will receive plenty of invitations to join those you love in their space. People are more likely to reveal their inner world to you when you let them take the initiative to share their life with you rather than feeling like they are being too pushed to do so. It is tempting as an Aries to push for more territory. That is a natural instinct with your sign. Just beware of the boundary lines and your relationships will flow more smoothly.

What if you are the person experiencing the space invasion from someone else? To transform this past-life pattern, you need to reclaim your territory. It will take some practice to find the confidence to establish a clear sense of boundary. It is not that you want to keep people out of your space. It is that you need your territorial rights recognized and respected. An Aries like yourself thrives on being assertive for your own ideas and needs. It is as important as the air you breathe. When you declare your space as your very own, it makes it easier to establish balance in your important relationships. It brings your identity into full focus and truly empowers you.

Extreme Competitiveness

This past-life karmic pattern can be resolved through becoming more sensitive to how your actions impact others. This is a type of energy that when directed in a positive way toward your goals is wonderful. It only takes redirecting this part of your natural competitive expression with greater awareness. There will be occasions when you are so forcefully convinced your ideas are the best that you can turn people off. If you stay patient and think before acting on impulse, you will win great appreciation from those people you want to bring closer in your life. Your Aries strength can arouse a competitive spirit from people. Competition can empower you. Overpowering someone constantly to get your needs met can be transformed into a win-win philosophy.

Sabotaging a Relationship

The sabotaging a relationship pattern can be overcome by being willing to take the risk to stay longer in a relationship that has promise of a solid future. You could be surprised that establishing a commitment with someone is the path to healing this past-life pattern. You and a partner might decide in the end the relationship needs to be ended or perhaps it may remain a friendship. The important thing is that you are releasing a pattern by going in a new direction. It will become a learning experience and convince you that a deeper commitment will give you the insight not to leave a good relationship before you give it a fair chance. If this pattern is reoccurring in this lifetime, it might be due to a feeling of divine discontent, meaning you are in search of a perfect person. It could take some reality testing to find your way to accept there is no perfect person. A fear of a relationship failing as it begins can be brought under control by developing a positive attitude. Your belief in your ability to work together with a lover gains strength if you choose to stay long enough in a relationship to let it reveal itself.

Misguided Anger

The misguided anger past-life pattern requires a clearer channeling of your powerful emotions. When used as a weapon to force your opinions on others, anger has a disruptive effect on relationships. Trusting that you can openly negotiate with someone for what you need is a better path to choose. Compromise is often the ticket to getting your own goals supported. Returning the favor by helping someone else achieve their own goals gets you the same help in return. Anger used to intimidate others is better turned into working passionately to achieve mutual understanding in your social interactions.

Another possible side of this pattern is hiding your anger over a situation that can potentially explode onto the scene of an unrelated circumstance. That held-back anger is sure to make itself known in ways you might not be able to control. It is better to let your views be known even if they don't always seem well received by others. It takes the wrong intensity out of your emotions when you are more open with people. This allows for a more balanced way of expressing how you feel.

Promises Not Delivered

The promises not delivered past-life pattern is less of a pull on you if you are more reasonable about your capabilities. Sometimes the restlessness inherent in a fire sign like Aries will distract you from finishing a plan. If you anticipate a delay in what you have pledged to accomplish for someone, it helps to let them know in advance to avoid disappointing them. Communication is valuable in keeping others on the same page with you. The more you live up to your promises, the more people will do the same for you.

It is possible another feature of this pattern can emerge in your life, which is attracting people who don't follow through on promises. In other words, you frequently allowed this to happen to you in past incarnations. Making sure you assertively call people out on this behavior goes far in resolving this pattern.

The Aries Reward from Solving Karmic Patterns

"I Won't Back Down" is a song by the American rock star Tom Petty. There are occasions when an Aries will be asked by the universe to rise above their fear of adversity to move assertively toward a new goal. Facing the challenge presented by a karmic pattern is something you can accomplish. Each step forward might be accompanied by two steps back in resolving a past-life pattern. If you persist on your quest to overcome a karmic pattern, you will summon the Aries warrior courage to emerge from the fiery spirit of your sign. It does take some fortitude to face a karmic pattern. Each successful step along your life journey toward a new understanding of a past-life pattern empowers you.

If you identified with any of the Aries karmic patterns discussed, try not to worry. The main thing is becoming more aware of any pattern that has followed you into this lifetime. It does take some effort and determination to change a pattern into a more positive part of your self-expression.

A patient pursuit in dealing with a karmic pattern may not be easy for your inner restlessness. Taking the time to retrain your mind by obtaining a more productive expression of a past-life pattern pays dividends. You will find greater fulfillment in all your relationships.

TWO
TAURUS: THE BUILDER

Dates: April 20 to May 20

Element: Earth

Strengths: Stamina, patience, calming influence

Challenges: Stagnation, stubbornness, lack of initiative

Karmic Relationship Primary Shadow: Too attached to fixed perceptions

Key to Transforming Karmic Patterns: Becoming more flexible

The Taurus Current-Life
Relationship Landscape

If you were born under the sign of Taurus, you like people who don't rush you into a relationship. If you are already in a committed partnership, you appreciate someone supporting your goals. In traditional astrology the keyword phrase for your sign is "I have." People who are generous with their resources warm your mind and heart. You feel closer to individuals who value your ideas and insights. Being able to celebrate milestones in your life with a special person is a deep desire.

You tend to value friendship but grow impatient with those who take too much from you and give little in return. If your trust is betrayed, it is difficult to continue to want the offender in your life. You can display a wonderful way of going the extra mile to help a close friend in need of your help.

Your values must be respected by others. People don't have to adopt your belief system, but they gain your admiration if they don't try to push their own worldview on you. Finding a middle ground of mutual acceptance brings a peaceful and easy-flowing feeling.

You came into this life to form alliances with others without endless friction. Your persistence to make a relationship a success comes from a tenacious mind. Knowing when you have done all that is possible to keep a bond strong with a person comes with wisdom gained through experience. You might be perceived as someone who does not give up on a friendship during times of adversity.

People not afraid to show their passion in living their life quickly come into your awareness. It wakes up your own passion senses and stimulates your creativity. Someone paying attention to your emotional and sensual needs finds entry into your inner world. Feeling comfortable with people relaxes your mental energies.

The Taurus Past-Life Karmic Relationship Patterns

Past-life memories claim a resting place in our consciousness. These energies at times weave their way into our current life. You may feel a connection with some of the Taurus past-life patterns that will be discussed. If there are any that particularly strike a chord with you, don't let this bother you. Each of us has past-life themes that have gained entry into our current incarnation. Think of it as a learning experience and an opportunity to make a course correction. It is your chance to gain greater insight into a past-life shadow that wants to be brought out into the healing light.

As a Taurus, your consistent determination to transform the negative pull of a pattern into an empowering ally can become a reality. It does take a certain amount of practice to overcome a past-life pattern. Don't get discouraged if a pattern seems to reemerge in your life no matter your effort. At some point your movement through a pattern will occur. Think of this like you would strengthening a muscle in your body. You are empowering your mind and inner spirit as you acknowledge a pattern is active in your life.

Low Self-Esteem

If at times you are sensing that your self-esteem in a relationship has taken a downward motion, it could be a trend from past incarnations. This does not mean in all your past lives you had low self-worth. It could be certain people have a way of awakening this pattern, sending your self-esteem on a downward spiral. This past-life pattern can suddenly manifest like a shadow and can feel foreign to your usual way of relating with people.

It is very possible you are attracting individuals who have a way of negating your positive energy. This can be a past-life pattern operating on a subconscious level that manifests suddenly. That part of you looking for a person to support your goals is strong within you. When you are in relationships that stand in the way of your longing for mutual acceptance, they are tests to hang on to your self-esteem.

I Need Peace

There are people who bring out our intensity. Some of them make great partners and lovers. Passion can be a beautiful thing. If you are regularly in relationships that are sparring contests, it can grow old. This past-life pattern is in contradiction to the natural fondness for serenity in the soul of a Taurus. It isn't that a temporary quarrel with someone is a big problem, but living in a world of extreme tension with someone wears down your mental and emotional energy. An argument that goes on over an extended time period with no resolution in sight causes resentment.

Venus is the ruling planet of your Taurus slice of the zodiac pie. This planet thrives on being able to compromise. If you can't find equal territorial rights in a relationship with someone, feeling at ease is a challenge. Your Taurus nature needs to know the give and take is balanced. Otherwise, you will find yourself mentally or physically pulling away from a person who is a thorn in your side and causes you great stress.

Fixed Attitudes

Your sign has a strong maintaining ability that can help you outlast challenges and at times defies the odds. When you are determined to make a goal a success, your mind grows in intensity. If this pattern works its way into your relationships, that focusing power you adopt can backfire. How might this occur? Your ideas could lack flexibility, which makes communication breakdowns with others a great possibility. This past-life pattern may lie dormant until you are in relationships with people who are not good at accepting change. The chemistry in such a relationship can come to a grinding halt with neither of you willing to budge.

Fixed perceptions you are not willing to adjust can isolate you from the closeness you seek. Another way this pattern manifests is getting into relationships with individuals with tendencies to look at situations one-sided. That one side is what is best for them. This does not make for much teamwork when you need a reasonable partner. If you are with someone refusing to listen to your input about serious plans that need involvement from both of you, the result will disappoint you.

Lost Dreams

Each of us comes into this life with intuition that can guide us to dream of a better future. If this past-life shadow energy becomes activated, it might find you too willing to please others. When this occurs, your passion to pursue your own unique goals could suffer a setback. If you are in partnerships in which someone is constantly talking you out of pursuing a growth-promoting activity, you can miss out on a mentally invigorating experience.

This can be a recurring pattern from past lives that has worked its way in from your memory bank. You might not realize on a conscious level that you are engaged in this pattern. It is possible you could feel as though you are in a bad dream if too much of the time you let others step on your plans to make important changes in your life. That Taurus willpower of yours gets weakened if you surrender to the viewpoint of someone unable to share your need for a better today and tomorrow.

Possessiveness

If this past-life pattern becomes too active, you may find yourself leaning toward becoming too bossy and even controlling. Why might this happen? It could be caused by not trusting people or more likely caused by certain individuals having a way of activating this tendency from within you. Their behaviors make you feel suspicious of their actions. It can be a fear of not being in control of situations that brings you into this past-life pattern. Taurus instincts want to keep relationships stable. It might be that some individuals make you feel like you must be in control.

The other side of this pattern is that you might be attracting people who are too possessive of you. It is their manipulative behavior that can have a smothering effect. You could be afraid of losing this person if you call them out on their behavior. This will eventually give you a feeling of being trapped in a limiting relationship. This is not saying all your past lives were like this. It is only revealing that this is a pattern you could have brought into this incarnation to leave behind.

Clash of Values

This is a past-life pattern that comes to the surface in relating to others whose values are at odds with your own. It has more to do with each of you not being able to clearly communicate a need for mutual acceptance of what is important to you. Respecting one another's need for individual self-expression is usually at the root of this tension. In an incarnation when you have experienced a key insight that you need to move in a new creative direction, this can cause a disruption with a partner. Your own passion to make choices that bring new growth might be perceived inaccurately by others. If you can't find the middle ground to get the freedom to be yourself, a power struggle results. This in itself is natural to occur. It can be a problem if you are expected to act like you have not had a new idea of what inspires you in life.

If you have to constantly hide your new life interests from someone, it does start to wear on your energy levels. After all, you have to be you. An authentic you is what nourishes that Taurus sense of fulfillment. If you can't live out what you value, you will always feel like something is missing.

Fear of Adversity

Your Taurus nature gravitates toward seeking pleasant life experiences. That is a good thing to want in life. None of us can afford to reject feelings of inner peace and serenity. All relationships will go through some ups and downs periodically. If this past-life pattern pays you a visit, you might find yourself leaving a promising partnership too early. Friction in a relationship may bombard your nervous system with too much anxiety. This isn't saying to stay in a relationship that is bad for your health. But if you vacate a relationship too soon due to the first experience of a disagreement, you might be giving up on a potentially good thing.

If you stay with someone to work out a problem, it can prove to be a valuable learning experience for each of you. You will get stronger when facing adversity in a more direct way. This pattern weakens in its intensity when not letting it worry you. There are no perfect people, which means there are no perfect relationships. If you run away from adversity, it has a tendency to often appear bigger than it is in reality.

Stuck in the Past

If emerging in the current incarnation, this pattern is linked to a few different possibilities. One is you can't shake the attachment to a past relationship. Disappointment over the end of a relationship that you truly are still attached to can obstruct a new love from starting. Taurus has more stamina than most signs to keep feeling a relationship can be fixed even when a partner has left. The longing to find someone who is like a past lover can cause misperceiving the opportunity when meeting someone new.

The past can even be subconsciously looking for a soul mate who resembles or reminds you of a past-life love. This is only a problem if you want a person to live up to unreasonable expectations. You may not be aware that it is a past-life love partner who is shadowing your perceptions when looking at a new potential love experience. In this instance you are not allowing the current life to unfold in a way that will let you have fulfillment with a new individual.

Living in Shallow Water

Developing emotional depth in relating to others takes time. When activated, this past-life pattern finds you pulling back from someone to hide your feelings. Usually a lack of trust is at the root of this pattern. It is not so unusual when a relationship is beginning not to reveal our deeper self. As the bond between two people gets stronger, there is a foundation on which to build trust. It could be that someone is causing you to avoid the deeper emotional waters. If this repeats itself on an ongoing basis, swimming to the deeper end of the emotional water is a problem. You could be attracting people who cause this past-life pattern to surface. Their own unwillingness to talk about the feeling side of life could be the reason for only wanting to get your toes wet emotionally. It could be that in some past lives it was difficult for you to find a partner willing to open up their emotional world to you. If this occurs again when you are involved with a person for a long duration of time, you will sense that you deserve a closer connection emotionally.

Cannot Live with or without You

This past-life pattern usually can be traced back along a trail of either indecision or possibly looking for too much perfection in people. The lack of decisiveness about relationships might be due to a hesitation about wanting to make a commitment. Being careful and patient is a wise thing to do, but always finding a reason that all people are not the right fit for you could be due to either a fear of commitment or feeling there has to be that just right person waiting for you to find them.

If you find that this pattern hits the mark with you, it is just saying this is a theme that followed you into this incarnation. There can be a sense of feeling like you are close to a person yet want to suddenly distance yourself at the same time. This pattern can give you a sensation that you are in a constant struggle of seeking intimacy with someone and at the same time desiring space. Making peace with these opposites is the challenge.

Too Guarded

If activated, this past-life pattern can find you feeling too protective of yourself and blocking anyone from getting too close. It is a good idea to be sure you can trust someone before letting them into your inner world, but if you always close the door to letting someone get to know you, it will make a solid relationship hard to create. It does take a bit of taking a risk to allow for greater intimacy into your life. There is no rule that says you have to move fast into a relationship. This pattern lessens in intensity when you let go of your fear of letting a person form a bond with you based on trust.

Another way this pattern manifests itself is if you are inviting people who are too guarded into your life. In other words, it is a past-life pattern that could take the form of encountering people who hide their true selves too much of the time. They are mirroring something you came into this life to work on and transform. Sometimes the thing each of us needs to overcome from a past life is presented to us in the people we meet. Look at it as an opportunity to see the pattern in someone else and not something you want to bring into your own life.

Boundary Confusion

Your Taurus earth sign can be very pragmatic about what you look for in friends and lovers. There is a need to keep your feet on solid ground even when falling in love. If this past-life pattern is awakened in the current incarnation, your boundaries can become blurred. This could result in not getting a clear picture of how to define a relationship. You might find yourself in a state of emotional confusion when your boundaries are not clear. Your life might feel out of control, not in the way you would prefer. Sometimes the cause of this past-life pattern is wanting too much from someone or the partner having unrealistic expectations. Your sense of personal empowerment is less if you feel the territory you need to be yourself has been compromised. The greater the closeness the greater the potential for this pattern to emerge if there is an absence of clear communication.

Altered Perceptions: Taurus Paths to Transforming Karmic Relationship Patterns

Releasing a karmic pattern feels like a breath of wholesome fresh air has replenished your mind, body, and soul. It might even give you a sense of a powerful rebirth. Your relationships have a new path to be fulfilling experiences. In some ways you are rewarding yourself with a new gift each time you find the determination to overcome the negative pull of a past-life pattern. The shadow force, when brought into the light of a new clearer awareness, is wonderful. The potential for greater harmony in your relationships becomes a reality. If one of the discussed karmic patterns rings true for you, do not worry. On the contrary, hopefully you will see there are other positive ways to express these energies. Often a karmic pattern is hidden from our conscious awareness. It can take practice to get better at not letting a past-life pattern interfere with happiness you want to achieve in this lifetime. The first step is recognizing when a karmic pattern is active in your life. It is then you will begin to hold the key to open the door to greater self-discovery and create relationships filled with a harmonizing attunement.

Low Self-Esteem

If the low self-esteem pattern sounds like it followed you into this incarnation, then you need to get good at rewarding yourself with whatever it takes to get you to a higher level. It does not need to happen all at once. It will take some of that Taurus patience and persistence your sign is known to have. You will be surprised to see how quickly you can start to move in a new direction if you slowly take the first steps in a new positive direction. You will feel a renewed creative spark when believing that you deserve to bring more fulfilling experiences into your life.

People having negative perceptions of you need not occupy your mental nature. You could need to get tougher mentally to ward off the input from others that lowers your self-worth. This process of not accepting others' negative opinions of you will become a normal part of your everyday operating in the world. You did not come into this life to repeat this pattern. Stay thinking positive and you will leave this pattern in your forward-moving tracks.

I Need Peace

This pattern might only need a slight tweak in your perceptions to get on a smoother road to harmony. Some intensity in life is normal and often is a catalyst to launch new goals. A Taurus like yourself tends to get overwhelmed when there is constant discord in your everyday life. Being in relationships that have little peace makes life not as much fun. Sometimes this pattern will find its way into an incarnation if you have a partner in the habit of creating a crisis. If you can stay away from people wanting to escalate the tension too much of the time, you will be happier. Seeking out people who truly want an equal partnership is one sure way to balance out this pattern. A winning formula to overcome this pattern is surrounding yourself with individuals who want to achieve harmony rather than ones that are looking to create struggles with no understanding of how to put out a fire they started.

Fixed Attitudes

The fixed attitudes pattern is right in your wheelhouse to turn into a more productive energy. Taurus can stubbornly resist making changes—that is true. Then again, you have a get-down-to-business drive to put into motion a new insight. If this past-life pattern tries to zero in on you, the best remedy is flexibility. It is a sure way to get the communication flowing with people. You need not compromise your own goals. The likely result of showing an open mind is getting more support for your ideas.

This pattern can mean that in some past lives you had to deal with people having closed minds on a regular basis. If this is a repeat performance, it can be frustrating. If individuals are trying to interfere with your future plans with their own rigid opinions too much of the time, you will need to find the confidence to stay focused on your goals. The main message here is to remember to be willing to change directions and stay open to new learning.

Lost Dreams

If too active in your current life, this pattern can be overcome in more than one way. The first thing to remember is your sign was gifted at birth with a great amount of patience. You might feel at times that you have to outlast the influence of this past-life pattern by maintaining a forward momentum to reach a goal. Having dreams of a better tomorrow is something to be cherished. You could need to express your intention to make a dream come true with greater force. This may require you to learn to not let outside opinions distract you away from what you want to accomplish.

Often it is our intuition showing us how to have a dream to reach toward and guiding us to make it come true. When you are in those moments of doubt, don't despair. That dream or goal giving you inspiring confidence to walk your talk is never far away. You can't always please others, which can take you away from your most heartfelt dreams. You could need to put yourself first even if it feels uncomfortable to do. Believing in your ability is a big part of the path to letting the universe make a dream come true.

Possessiveness

The possessiveness past-life pattern orbits around trust issues. You need to give others the same amount of freedom you want for yourself in relationships. This pays great dividends in terms of feeling that you have a bond with someone based on trust. Growing overly possessive of someone takes energy from you that could be more productively expressed. Having the confidence to let go of a need to be possessive is a liberating experience. The love and closeness you desire flourish when you transcend this pattern.

Attracting people who have strong controlling tendencies requires you to stand your ground. There is a possibility you will need to distance yourself from people with extreme possessive behaviors. A relationship colored with shared power is the road to personal fulfillment. When you see you don't need to tolerate individuals not respecting your independence, you are gaining the insight needed to make this past-life pattern go for a long sleep.

Clash of Values

This past-life pattern usually requires clear communication with lovers, friends, and family members. Sometimes to keep the peace the wise policy is to agree to disagree. Having ways you and a partner perceive the world independently stimulates growth for each of you. The exchange of knowledge from different points of view can be mentally stimulating. A mutual respect for what each other values builds trust. When you do come together on a shared plan, it will have that much more power behind it.

What you value in life can't be compromised if it is an important belief system that fills you with inspiration. There will be new insights that could rock the boat in a relationship. How you introduce and explain your new thinking is important to ensure it is well received. Timing when to reveal new ideas to others is something else to keep in mind. There may be a person who might try to talk you out of a new life direction you choose to walk. If it is a goal you greatly value, there is no price worth not pursuing it. If this pattern has occurred in this life, it likely has been part of your past-life history. Your Taurus personal empowerment is linked to what you value in life. It is as essential as the air you breathe.

Fear of Adversity

The fear of adversity pattern could awaken in you that in some past lives there are some memories embedded in your consciousness reminding you of struggles in relationships. Love and passion can at times bring out a certain amount of intensity in a relationship. Your Taurus natural tendency is to seek tranquility in all aspects of your everyday life. If you are in a relationship that you like and learn to flow with the ups and downs, the bond will grow stronger. People tend to need one another when facing challenges together.

This pattern might come to the surface when you fear an argument will cause you to lose a partner. There are times it is good to bring an issue you have with a person out into the open. What appears to be a problem brings you closer together through clear communication. Your relationships can go through a rebirth through taking on adversity in a direct manner. Your ruling planet is Venus, which gives you a capacity to be diplomatic when tackling a relationship issue. Finding the courage to stay in a relationship when the going gets tough can bring you a sense of empowerment. The milestones you can celebrate with the right partner are worth the time walking through the challenges together.

Stuck in the Past

This pattern need not keep you from exploring new relationships. The past can be a great teacher offering us wisdom. It can guide us to learn from our mistakes so we don't repeat them. But you do need to be careful not to let it rule your thinking. If you allow yourself the freedom to release the hold of a past relationship partner, you open the door to finding someone new who will be a better fit for what you need in the present. That same Taurus energy that has been focused too much in the rearview mirror only needs to be aimed in a forward direction.

You have to buy into the reality that you deserve people in your life who reflect who you are and want to become. It takes some courage to move ahead even if part of you is still looking back. The reward is much greater if you close the door on the past. You came into this life to form fulfilling partnerships. The Taurus craving for love and intimacy is within your grasp when you relinquish the past.

Living in Shallow Water

When you feel safe in relationships with people, this living in shallow water past-life pattern is less likely to get activated. You may have sensed early on in your life that individuals you trust are the ones to whom you reveal your deepest feelings. You are happier on every level when in the company of people feeling free to share their own inner world. There will always be some individuals who make us feel cautious before ever trusting them. This is actually a wise way to operate.

Staying clear of getting too close to people who never talk about their emotions could be a wise policy. Trying to form a deeper bond with these individuals is difficult if they insist on staying in the shallow water. If it is greater depth from a person you want, then not settling for less is the more expansive path to personal happiness, love, and harmony.

Cannot Live with or without You

Feeling comfortable in a relationship does often require some time. This pattern will test your patience as you determine if you are in the right relationship for you. There is no need for guilt if you should decide to not remain in a love or friendship type of relationship. If activated, this past-life pattern can be overcome. It can create some anxiety as you release the pull of this shadowy energy. If you are with someone who seems to cause you indecision, it will take your objectivity to do what is in your best interest. Passion is a wonderful thing, but obsession to be with a person actually takes away your power. If you make peace with this past-life pattern, your sense of inner peace is the reward. It could take an honest determination to define what you really feel you need in a relationship to find harmony.

Looking for perfection in yourself or someone else can be frustrating. You will be happier when in relationships that give you a feeling of stability. A Taurus like yourself likely wants to know a partner is working as hard as you are at creating a fulfilling relationship. You will not be as happy if you are always wondering if you made the right decision in staying or leaving a relationship. Listen to that inner voice trying to guide you to choose people who give you a reassured feeling they want to be a trusting and loving partner. It is then you will know you have chosen the right path forward.

Too Guarded

The too guarded pattern usually means you are being too protective of yourself. Scrutinizing others before letting them get close is a wise thing to do. It is only if you always keep a barrier around you that there is a chance you will miss out on a good relationship. Sometimes it is the past emotional pain endured from this life or past lives that can keep you putting out a stiff arm in the face of people. At some point in time taking the risk to let an individual come into your world can be the first step in rising above this pattern. You don't have to reveal your inner world quickly. A Taurus likes to move at a calm and steady pace into new experiences. When you open yourself to letting down your guard, a bond with a special someone can become a reality.

If you seem to attract people who keep their guard up, it might be the universe trying to give you a glimpse of how this pattern can keep you from the happiness you desire. The key thing to remember is the current incarnation does not require you to repeat this pattern yourself. When you find that balance between your need to guard your private world and comfortably sharing intimacy, you will never have to worry about this pattern.

Boundary Confusion

This pattern shows that romantic love has a particular way of blurring the boundaries with a lover. Any relationship that stirs up emotional intensity can challenge you to keep your territorial lines clearly defined. There is nothing wrong with being extra supportive of lovers, friends, and family members when called upon. If this past-life pattern has presented itself as a problem, then you do need to begin to balance dependency needs. You will feel more empowered when getting a handle on this pattern. Your relationships will feel more rewarding.

People in your life who have trouble understanding boundaries benefit from your own assertiveness to claim your space. As you grow comfortable with traveling in your own lane, your behavior has a secondary impact of showing someone else their own lane. There is a pretty good chance your creative vitality and mental energy will be recharged when you rise above this pattern.

The Taurus Reward from
Solving Karmic Patterns

Patience and determination color your Taurus Sun sign with the right stuff to deal positively with karmic patterns. The path through any past-life pattern does have some challenges. If it looks like a tall mountain to climb, don't get discouraged. The relationship fulfillment you can claim when rising above a karmic pattern is a wonderful reward.

Each of us has some karmic patterns that came with us into this lifetime. You are not alone when it comes to becoming aware of a pattern and the need to deal with it. The new energy you will feel when healing any of these patterns is amazing. It might even surprise you how your new insights help you in all areas of your life.

Your relating to others gets an energized boost through healing a past-life pattern. A brave new world awaits you when walking in paths that promise new growth. Your vision will get empowered with an attitude filled with a magical self-confidence as you harmonize your understanding of a past-life pattern.

THREE
GEMINI: THE COMMUNICATOR

Dates: May 21 to June 21

Element: Air

Strengths: Communication, teaching, adaptability

Challenges: Easily bored, losing sense of direction, negative thinking

Karmic Relationship Primary Shadow: Not trusting insights

Key to Transforming Karmic Patterns: Being open to new growth

The Gemini Current-Life Relationship Landscape

If you were born under the sign of Gemini, you came into this life to relate to a wide variety of people. Maybe it could just as well be said your curiosity drives you to explore the minds of others. Sharing ideas with a lover, friend, business associate, or family member is a stimulating experience. Being in relationships with an individual who likes to openly share what is on their mind appeals to you. Those who hide their thoughts from you on a continual basis worry you. Your energetic way of wanting to seek new learning attracts people to you.

Travel on the mental and physical levels is in your sign's DNA. There is a desire to find people who are open to the way you perceive the world around you. A person does not have to agree with all your ideas. You only want to know they are listening to you.

There are times you will need to change a life direction quickly. Your mind lives in the moment. Your closest allies in life like that about you. You could grow frustrated with those who try to limit your options. The more roads to success and happiness in your imagination the more fulfilled you feel.

Your mind has a tendency to work fast. Individuals who connect with this part of you seem to understand you. You want to be accepted as a free thinker. Some might find you aloof. You like to think of this as mentally processing life as it happens.

The Gemini Past-Life
Karmic Relationship Patterns

If you identify with any of the past-life memories in this book, it is better to observe them as learning experiences. Each of our signs has brought something from past incarnations for us to balance. The information in this book is meant to serve as a guide to helping you integrate a past-life pattern into the current life in a more harmonious way. In gaining awareness of a past-life pattern, you start the process of a new self-discovery.

As a Gemini, your piercing intellect can navigate through any past-life pattern with new insight. It can take some practice to find the inner strength to keep moving in a clearer direction regarding a past-life pattern. The following patterns lessen in their influence as you gain the confidence to transform them into illuminating energies. Remember to enjoy the journey in rising above a past-life pattern, as this is the lighthouse that will always be there for you.

Hiding behind the Intellect

If this past-life pattern becomes an active part in your relating to others, your intellect could conceal your emotions in relationships too much of the time. As a Gemini, your first impulse is to make use of a strong mind. This is your primary way of connecting with people. In your closest relationships your mental side could become a problem if it will not allow you to express your feelings. There are times you may not even realize you are doing this. There are occasions when a pattern has become activated that it acts out like it is a natural part of our thought processes. A lover, friend, or family member may perceive you as distancing yourself purposely. It is not unusual when first entering a new relationship to not reveal your innermost world. But as time goes on, if you are not willing to communicate any feelings, it could cause a lack of trust in relating to others. Gemini is what is known as an air sign, which features a great reliance on the mental side of life. Crossing over into feelings can be a challenge. If you never risk being honest about your emotional nature, it could make closeness difficult with others.

Mixed Signals

This pattern has more than one cause. One way it can manifest is through self-doubt. It causes a lack of decisiveness and can interfere with having clear communication with others. It can make a commitment with someone a real challenge. Another path this pattern can take is purposely giving misleading information to others. It does make giving a clear picture of what you need from someone confusing. It will feel like you are going around in cloudy circles in defining a relationship clearly. If you continue going down this road, it can keep you from having relationship fulfillment. If you are wanting support for your goals from others, it may not be there when you need it most.

Yo-Yo

If activated in your life, this pattern is acted out by making someone feel close and then pushing them suddenly away. It could be an unpredictable behavior that suddenly takes place. You could be surprised yourself when this occurs. A past-life pattern can hang around in the background of our conscious awareness. Then when a situation presents itself, like you are not sure just how close you want to be with someone, this pattern comes quickly into being. What causes this? It is possible you don't yet trust that a relationship is really what you need at the present time. This pattern is a problem if you feel you have met someone special but can't seem to stop this pattern from getting in the way of your happiness. Your mind does work fast and may at times jump to conclusions that a relationship is moving at a quicker pace than you find comfortable. There is nothing wrong with this reasoning. But if this is an ongoing and regular event in your life, it is likely this pattern interfering in a way that could be limiting your chances for relationship harmony.

Emotional Burnout

This past-life pattern for a Gemini like yourself will usually make its entrance if you have an ongoing roller-coaster ride of emotions in a relationship. Emotional turmoil with someone you care about begins to wear on your mental strength. If you can't find emotional stability in a relationship, it is painful. This could be a leftover pattern from some past lives, in which you could not find the inner peace you so badly needed. You don't have to repeat the pattern. But if you stay emotionally confused, it makes for not much fun in any of your relating to others.

It could be you find yourself in a relationship with a person who has a tendency to push your emotional buttons quickly. If you stay in relationships that lack clear communication, this pattern has a bigger opportunity to emerge into your life. Your intuition may feel stifled in relationships that take too much of you giving too much emotional support and not enough receiving. If the dependency needs get out of balance, you will sense something you need for fulfillment is missing.

Keeping You Guessing

This pattern is aggravating if it comes into play. When someone is hiding what they really want from you, it can create much anxiety in your life. Honest communication may be too absent. Gemini people don't mind surprises, as they keep life interesting. Being deceived by an individual's intentions is a whole other story. If you are trying to get close to someone but feel a wall around them, it does make it difficult to establish trust. It can grow frustrating to try to figure someone out as time goes on. It will test your patience, probably more than you want, if a person will not reveal what they want from you. The mystique and intrigue of meeting someone new can be exciting. But it wears thin if it stays at that level over a long time period. Intimacy could be out of reach, which can be disappointing if you stay stuck in this pattern. This could be a repeating past-life influence in which you get involved with people purposely misleading you.

Hidden Anger

A Gemini cannot hold back anger for extended periods without it eventually exploding right in front of you. It might even surprise you to see it all come out at once. You and all the people who are important to you are better off if you express your ideas in the moment. It is true some friction can result if you are direct with others. Your relationships do get empowered if you are openly assertive. Diplomacy can be woven into sensitive subjects. If you associate with friends and lovers who want you to tiptoe around them, the relationship probably won't last for long. Eventually you need to say what is on your mind. If you keep swallowing anger, it gets bigger and bigger inside you and is rough on your nervous system. Your verbal skills as a Gemini need to be displayed. If you are in a relationship with someone who causes you to deny your angry feelings over and over, this becomes problematic.

Endless Boredom

Every relationship needs some routine to stay grounded and maintain a sense of direction. One thing that can derail a relationship for a Gemini is boredom. You need people in your life who are adaptable and don't fear change, or at least you require a partner who gives you the freedom to keep your mind stimulated. "Variety is the spice of life" is a mantra never too far from the Gemini mind. Exploring new ideas and areas of interest together with a lover keeps the relationship growing. If you remain in relationships that grow stale, this pattern will weave its way into your life. You will possibly become extremely restless and begin to doubt if your relationship can sustain your need for more vibrancy. When this karmic shadow presented itself in past lives, you found yourself feeling the urge to go where the grass seemed greener.

Looking for the Negative

If this pattern gains too much access to your thinking, there is a tendency to find fault with people even if there are no real problems. You do have an analytical tendency that can look for perfection that could be impossible for someone to fulfill. It may be that you put yourself under a microscope too often, which causes a disruption in your relationships because you demand too much from yourself. If you lose sight of thinking positively, it does tend to make finding the harmony with others difficult. Your mind will create problems to sabotage the happiness you want to have if this pattern becomes too much of a companion.

Another way this past-life pattern can surface is being in relationships with people who display this pattern. If you deny this is occurring, you will continue to attract this type of person into your life. Sometimes this happens when you don't trust your insights. You may catch glimpses that a person is lost in negativity but refuse to confront a partner. This could be a past-life pattern you have come into this life to transcend. You are getting an opportunity to see firsthand that this is a pattern you want to keep at a great distance.

False Assumptions

The Gemini mind can move at great speed. If this past-life pattern gets activated as a dominant force, you could come to wrong conclusions about people. You could lose your objectivity by not taking the time to step away from situations. Focusing excessively on what could go wrong could cause this to occur. It is possible you keep expecting someone to fall back into behaviors you asked them to stop. Often it is emotional confusion that can cloud your mental perceptions and be the cause of this pattern. You have a great capacity to find your way out of this pattern, but if your mind gets caught up in assuming people will not be able to act in the ways you need them to perform, your relationships will fall short of your hope for fulfillment.

Over Worrying

There is attention to detail in Mercury-ruled signs like Gemini. If you become too obsessive in worrying about the little things, it can aggravate you in your relationships. It may not be obvious you are even caught in this pattern. If you maintain a vision of what you like in a relationship in a reasonable way, this pattern lessens in its intensity. If you are spending too much of the time thinking about how to create a perfect partnership or friendship, it eats away at your happiness. There is divine discontent at the root of this past-life influence. This means it is a difficult challenge to accept that each of us has some faults. There is no perfect soul mate in the world. Working through the problems is part of the deal. Accepting this is not easy if this pattern gets too active in your life.

Communication Breakdown

There probably is nothing worse for a Gemini like yourself to experience than a serious communication breakdown in a relationship. This is a pattern that occurs when you are in a relationship with someone and a wall appears between the two of you. Usually this happens if you and a partner have stopped hearing what the other is saying. It is as though you both are speaking in a foreign language. It can be hurtful if you sense someone has stopped truly listening to you. Sometimes this pattern comes into being if you lose your patience with others.

You might encounter this pattern in the form of being in a relationship with a person who cuts off communication at the slightest sign of a disagreement. It might be that you are getting a chance to see the pattern being exhibited by someone else. It is an opportunity to perceive this theme as a behavior you no longer choose to adopt for yourself. Sometimes a past-life pattern will present itself in the actions of a person we are trying to get to understand better. If you engage in the same way of acting out this pattern, you will not find the harmony you seek.

Too Much Criticism

Criticism is a delicate subject in most relationships. As a past-life pattern, it can creep in when you least expect it. This pattern can drive a deep wedge between you and others if it is overused. If it becomes a tool to hurt those you love, it is a very negative energy that drives people away. Tension becomes the norm rather than a closer form of intimacy if criticism gets out of control. There are times you have to accept your differences with someone to keep the peace.

If you happen to be the person receiving the brunt of criticism, it could hit a nerve in you. Why? It may be a past-life pattern that you came into this life to not overindulge in using. An individual regularly critical of your decisions could be pushing a past-life memory button within your consciousness. Failing to confront the individual can be a real drain on your energy.

Altered Perceptions: Gemini Paths to Transforming Karmic Relationship Patterns

A Gemini needs to know there are options to letting go of any karmic pattern. This is a key ingredient to your ability to gain the insight to get a pattern to release its grip on you. The freedom you will feel in facing a past-life shadow energy will energize your mind in empowering ways. Your creative energy will seem like it has been given a turbo boost. Your relationships could find clearer communication and greater intimacy. Rising above a karmic past-life pattern starts with small steps forward. Don't worry if you feel like you have taken a step backward. Your consistent effort to master a past-life pattern will eventually pay dividends.

If you recognize any of the karmic patterns as having been encountered in this incarnation, look at it as a learning experience. You will gain greater confidence in dealing with a pattern as you learn how to not let it interfere with the happiness you want in your relationships. Be patient. Chances are it will take some time to more productively channel a karmic pattern in a new positive direction. It could help you attract people to you who want to establish a fulfilling partnership. Remember that acknowledging a pattern is the beginning of walking on a new path with stimulating insights that will make the journey one that can bring personal and relationship fulfillment.

Hiding behind the Intellect

In this past-life pattern, it does not take a big tweak to solve the challenge of sharing more feelings. It is better for your overall mental and emotional balance to welcome those you want to bring closer into your inner world. The passion with a lover deepens when you open up about your emotional depth. Trust develops through taking the risk of allowing someone to get a clear picture of your emotions. You don't have to reveal all your secrets. Greater intimacy in your relationships is the reward for working your way through this pattern. Your communication skills are powerful and a tremendous asset. Your perceptions about people you feel comfortable with allow you a bridge to express feelings. Taking that first step in letting someone see the inner you is the path to releasing this pattern.

Mixed Signals

The mixed signals pattern could be linked to past incarnations in which you were in relationships that lacked clear definition. It does not mean all your past lives were like this. To avoid a repeat performance in acting out this pattern, you only need to give clear messages to others. The support for your goals gets strengthened when you communicate what you need from others clearly. You might have some self-doubt or don't feel deserving of a solid relationship. If you can move into a more positive frame of mind, this pattern will disappear.

It is possible you are in relationships that feature this pattern, meaning it is a partner with this influence. It is your chance to recognize this is happening and have your own insight that you don't want to go back into this pattern yourself. Being able to identify this pattern in others is your ticket out of this past-life energy.

Yo-Yo

The yo-yo pattern can be overcome after you have decided to give a relationship a chance. You will likely find if you don't distance yourself from someone with no warning, there is less friction with a partner. There is nothing wrong with wanting some space as needed. If you give advance warning when you need time alone, it lessens the interference of this pattern. You will find it is possible to have closeness and distance as needed if you take the time to communicate clearly. Chances are if you have the right people in your life, they will want some time to themselves to pursue their own goals. It is not unusual for Gemini individuals to need a certain amount of free time. You probably have multiple ideas to pursue that may take you away for periods of time from those you love and cherish. It is not that difficult to keep someone close. Let them know they are important even when you are apart. Stay supportive of the goals of a friend or lover and the intimacy is always present.

Emotional Burnout

The emotional burnout pattern can be navigated around if you remain vigilant about not letting it into your life. The more you insist on people working with you rather than against you, the more likely this past-life shadow will disappear from your life. It is easier to tune in to your intuition when your emotions are in balance. You have a strong mental nature as a Gemini. Your insights stay sharper when your emotional energy remains strong. There are going to be times when you and the important people in your life will be at odds over certain plans you have. This is only a problem if those differences begin to put a great strain on the relationship. Dependency needs with an equal give and take maintain the peace. With practice you can sense when emotional tension between you and others has reached too high a level. It helps to stay centered and grounded through taking walks, meditation, and whatever techniques you find that keep you happy and healthy.

Keeping You Guessing

This past-life pattern wastes too much energy if you can't get someone to reveal their expectations of you and what they really are looking for in a relationship. It is far better to let someone know how this is impacting you. If this pattern has been repeating, you probably need to be more assertive in getting a relationship to move faster in the direction you prefer. Sometimes this has more to do with a partner reluctant for some reason to make a commitment or at least clearly define the relationship. You are better off having a standard that will not allow for ongoing communication confusion. The more emotionally intense a relationship is, the more often you need to wear your business hat and find out more quickly what is someone's goal for your being together. It may come down to telling yourself a reality check is needed to get a clearer vision of how you fit into a relationship.

Hidden Anger

The hidden anger past-life pattern has to be dealt with if it comes into your current life scene. The Gemini nervous system is much better off when you make your ideas known in the moment. Anger is a raw emotion. You are an air sign, which features an intellect that stays clear when not holding back anger for extended time periods. Sometimes the fear of letting anger out is worse than trying to hide it. If you get good at not holding resentment toward someone due to stuffing down hurt feelings, your mental perceptions stay clear. You will have much more creative energy lined with a positive outlook when not giving in to this pattern. Your relationships get empowered and might even go through a rebirth when you ascend to higher ground in releasing this past-life influence.

Endless Boredom

The endless boredom pattern seems counterintuitive in every way for a Gemini. Relationships require people who to some degree keep you mentally stimulated. Otherwise storm clouds of inner restlessness circulate through your mind. If you are in a relationship with a stable partner who might have different life interests, you need the freedom to pursue activities that give you a sense of growth. If your friends and lovers share your desire for exploring new learning, you feel on top of the world. The key thing to remember to keep this pattern in check is to not let boredom be a frequent companion. When you are feeding your mind invigorating experiences, your relationships get an intimacy as well as a passion recharge.

Looking for the Negative

This pattern presents a challenge you are fully equipped to handle. Trusting your insights puts you in the driver's seat and this pattern in the rearview mirror. You are blessed with a powerhouse of a Gemini mind. You might need to dial back an intense search for perfection in yourself or others. Training your mind to think positive if needed comes with practice. When you see the cup at least half full, your relationships flow better. There is nothing like positive reinforcement to elevate your mind above the hold of this pattern.

If you are in relationships with those who tend too much of the time to have a negative outlook, it does weigh on your energy. If you don't deny you perceive this in others, it helps you create clarity in your relationships. It might even help a partner be happier if you engage the negative tendency in their thought processes. In reaching out for the positive energy in other people, your relationships walk on the path to harmony and fulfillment.

False Assumptions

The false assumptions pattern only requires you to go a little slower before drawing a final judgment about people. There are going to be occasions when your first perception will be very accurate. But a relationship that will stand the test of time might ask you to be patient. The first impressions of others may only be part of their persona or personal style. They likely are not revealing the deeper dimensions of who they are in the beginning. You have a mind that travels along fast brain circuitry. It only needs to go at a slower pace or give a relationship a closer look before jumping to conclusions. If you recognize this as a past-life pattern active in the present incarnation, you can overcome it by learning to be a good listener. Taking the time to participate in real communication with someone is the road to finding a true soul mate.

Over Worrying

This pattern is only needing you to channel your energy in more positive directions. If this sounds too difficult to accomplish, it really isn't. You have one of the most adaptable of the twelve astrological signs. This is quite an asset to use to deal with this past-life influence. You are happier and have greater vitality to enjoy your relationships when worry is kept to a minimum. Expecting perfection from yourself or others is not realistic. The big reward in rising above this pattern is attracting a great companionship with someone. You will feel mentally invigorated and will enjoy the intimacy you seek with a person when you practice putting excess worry away from you.

Communication Breakdown

Too much silence in a relationship does not usually work for a Gemini. The communication breakdown pattern feels like there is too much distance between you and someone. Finding the way back to peace, friendship, and love is closer than you might think. Listening to each other's mutual need to be heard is the first step. The passion and emotional support you desire could be faster to accomplish if some compromise is reached. There can be emotional intensity over hurt feelings causing the lack of talking things out. If you take the time to pause, you probably will gain a more objective view of situations. Your mind travels fast, and there will be times that slowing down your reaction time can help to resolve differences.

This pattern can present itself through people you know. The universe can work this way to give each of us a chance to get a view of how a pattern can manifest. The key thing here is that you are able to perceive this is a behavior you no longer want to wear yourself. When you speak from your heart and feelings, your words make others want to connect with you in magical ways.

Too Much Criticism

This pattern is easier to transform if you look for the positive in others first. There will be times you will not be happy with the actions of someone you love and will feel compelled to point out what bothers you. This is normal. If you can let some things go because nobody is perfect, you will find this past-life energy gets quieter. If the goal is finding harmony and love with someone and you keep that as the central focus, this pattern has a tendency to leave you alone. There is often an intense energy behind this pattern that, when directed toward creative pursuits and goals, will bring you great success. In other words, you are directing the energy to go along paths that are rewarding. It takes the pressure off the relationship.

If it is true you are in relationships with overly critical people as a repeating event, you are better off breaking the cycle. Either make it known you need more positive energy from people or avoid this type of person in your life. A past-life pattern can occur in the form of someone using this type of behavior. It is an opportunity to recognize this pattern in someone else and do your best to get out of its presence.

The Gemini Reward from
Solving Karmic Patterns

You are blessed with a mental strength that can guide you to navigate through any past-life pattern. Your adaptability is a gift to step back patiently and gain a new awareness whether you are first becoming aware of a past-life pattern or working your way through one. A karmic shadow comes into the light of a renewed sense of yourself as you gain a new understanding of this energy. It soon becomes a reality that a past-life pattern has no control over you. Your relationships find greater intimacy in releasing the hold of a pattern.

Don't worry if you connected with any of the patterns discussed. The first step in moving past a karmic energy is recognizing it. This helps give you the insight to turn the pattern into a more positive expression. Eventually, while you used to be a frequent flyer in a pattern, you are less and less in the habit of using it.

Your personal happiness is accelerated by rising above a past-life pattern. Your goals in life get brighter and your dreams get recharged. The love you want to share gets revitalized. Your relationships become enriched with an empowered wisdom that attracts the best life has to offer you.

FOUR
CANCER: THE PRESERVER

Dates: June 22 to July 21

Element: Water

Strengths: Empowered intuition, healer, caring

Challenges: Expressing emotions, trusting intuition, clarifying dependency needs

Karmic Relationship Primary Shadow: Fear of the unknown

Key to Transforming Karmic Patterns: Belief in your intuitive power

The Cancer Current-Life Relationship Landscape

If you were born under the sign of Cancer, finding people you can trust is part of your journey. You appreciate friends and lovers who support your goals without judging you. Your emotions might sometimes seem complex to people, but you likely accept this as a natural part of you. It may take some time for you to warm up to others before you let them really know you. You want your privacy to be respected but don't want those you love to stay away for too long.

The traditional astrology phrase for your sign is "I feel." Although, there are occasions when you want to rest your emotions and recharge your mental energy. You don't mind people depending on you but value those who let you lean on them in return.

Intimacy with a special person in your life gives you a sense of security. Those who understand your need for a peaceful home life become true friends. Connecting intuitively with people is a spiritual or mystical experience. You could meet individuals in surprising ways as if through a special synchronicity or a meaningful coincidence.

You have a caring side but probably don't want to reveal this too quickly. If you feel love for someone, your nurturing tendencies come out as powerful as a sunrise. If your feelings get hurt, you will spontaneously close off your inner world until you find it safe to come back out.

Your loyalty to others can last for a lifetime. Preserving a relationship you value is a heartfelt part of you. Building milestones with a lover through shared goals can become important to you. There are times your ideals will guide you to a unique plan for self-discovery. You need to do this as it empowers the bond you feel for others. You are attracted to people who act like they know how to express feelings.

The Cancer Past-Life Karmic Relationship Patterns

Everyone has past-life memories whether they are conscious of them or not. You probably will not identify with each of the karmic relationship patterns that will be discussed. If one or more of them speak to you, don't let it worry you. Each of us came here to grow and learn how to overcome past-life patterns. In recognizing a pattern you will begin to perceive how to make peace with it. It does take time and practice to gain a new understanding of this energy.

As a Cancer, your talent in processing experiences to see how they can fit into your life will help you in overcoming a past-life pattern. It is not unusual to feel like you are right back where you started in dealing with one of these patterns. That is okay. If you keep moving forward, sooner than you think the hold of a pattern will diminish right before your eyes.

I Feel Invisible

This past-life pattern can come to life for more than one reason. Sometimes it might feel like you have been taken for granted. It is as though you are expected to go along with the program of others. Your voice gets drowned out by the louder words of the people around you. You may be experiencing a pattern that has followed you into this incarnation if it sounds all too familiar. Your own dreams can be difficult to turn into reality. It may be true you are living out the hopes and wishes of someone else with your own kept behind the scenes. Your intuitive instincts get bottled up in this past-life influence. It can be your oversensitivity in not wanting to disappoint people that has you locked into this way of thinking.

Mood Swings

Being a water sign, the sign Cancer has the capacity to take you deep within yourself. There are occasions when someone might wonder what is on your mind. You may appear to be experiencing some type of mood suddenly. You probably think of this as a normal way to think things through. This pattern can be problematic if you are holding on to intense feelings without verbalizing a response to actions by others. You are more likely to explode toward someone if you have a habit of hiding your feelings. Moods can get out of control if you can't get a faster response time to situations that really need your honest input. Anger builds when you try to bury it and can bring out moody confrontations you want to avoid.

Dependency-Needs Imbalance

If this past-life pattern makes its presence felt, it takes the form of creating dependency issues. Every relationship requires an equal exchange in getting emotional support when needed. It is when you start to lose your own unique footing in a relationship that you can easily lose sight of your own goals. Sometimes this pattern occurs if you start leaning so heavily on someone that it throws the relationship off center, which translates to out of balance. If you expect someone to take on too much responsibility, it can take away from your sense of personal power.

There is another way this pattern takes shape. It is when you enable others to lean on you too heavily. The burden of this weight takes its toll on your mental strength. You may become very emotionally drained. It is possible this past-life pattern is coming at you through other people with dependency issues of their own. You are getting a chance here to see the pattern coming at you through others. If you enable the behavior to continue, it keeps you from the relationship harmony you would like to attain.

Walking on the Moon

Water signs like yourself have a strong emotional nature. You will occasionally find your intuitive expression well out in front of your mental articulation. If this pattern enters the scene, you could feel overwhelmed by the mental input from other individuals. Why does this happen? That powerful intuition you possess might sensitize you in a big way to the energy of people. The closer you get to someone in a relationship the more you may feel like you can't hold on to your own identity. It may be in some past lives this was a reality. Being involved with certain people could bring out this pattern as a repeat performance. You have a very active intuition that gets entangled with emotional confusion if you are in relationships that have an overwhelming impact on you.

Trouble Receiving

As a Cancer you are known to nurture and support those people you care about. You channel the universe as a giver of yourself to others. That is wonderful. If this pattern is too big a part of your everyday life in relationships, it denotes you are not as good at receiving for various reasons. One of them might be you don't feel deserving to receive love from others. It may be you are too busy trying to make everybody else feel good about themselves. You may have closed down importing love and affection. You excel at exporting your emotional support to people but have grown uncomfortable in receiving. It could come down to not wanting to become vulnerable. An inability to let people give back to you could prevent you from a more total experience of relationship fulfillment.

Hermit

A need for privacy is in the DNA of the sign Cancer. This past-life pattern materializes when you retreat into solitude as an escape. Everyone needs downtime from a busy life. Even space from our important people can be healthy. If it is more running away due to a fear of making a commitment to a relationship, then this pattern becomes a problem. It might be you have given up on finding closeness with someone due to not wanting to take the risk of being emotionally hurt. Staying in the confines of your own comfort zones can cause you to miss out on finding a compatible partner. It could be that memories in your consciousness from past lives have resurfaced from this pattern, causing a hesitation to trust that relationships will bring the happiness you desire.

Digging Up the Seed

This past-life pattern introduces itself to you in different ways. One is when you start out happy with a relationship but suddenly you want to slam on the brakes for no apparent reason. You begin to doubt it could possibly be true that you have met the right person. It usually comes down to overanalyzing the relationship. You begin to look for flaws that may or may not be there in the other person. The root of this pattern can be a fear that in the end the relationship will not succeed. Sometimes your emotional intensity crosses over into self-doubt that can cloud your perceptions. It might be that a failure to communicate your worries with a partner only serves to make this pattern a problem.

This pattern could manifest as picking relationship partners who display this behavior. It may come down to their own lack of faith in themselves that they can sustain a long-term relationship. This sometimes occurs to give you an opportunity to see the pattern in someone else without you having to repeat this behavior yourself.

Territorial Tension

To those born as a Sun sign Cancer, comfort zones are important. Home and to some degree having the privacy you prefer probably are highly valued. This pattern can come along in a relationship if someone disturbs your favorite ways of living your everyday life. You can feel confused about your identity if a person is trying to tell you how to live your life. You have good instincts for when people are invading your territorial rights, but they could be in a fog. Power struggles have a tendency to distance you from people. Your own goals and the way you want to approach them become a very personal need. Your need to claim some downtime from a relationship has to be honored for you to feel right and comfortable with a person. This could very well be a pattern lodged deep in your past-life memory bank.

Past Fears

Becoming comfortable with a new partner is challenging if you can't get let go of the past memories of previous relationships in the current incarnation that did not go well. This is an even deeper pattern when memories of unfulfilling relationships from past lives get activated. Your sign Cancer has a well-developed memory that at times will serve you well. If there is emotional pain baked into that memory, it can distort your perceptions of a current important person in your life. It might be a challenge to navigate around what has not made you happy previously in relationships to settle into new ones. It is very possible you are projecting onto someone images still in your mind from previous encounters from past incarnations that disappointed you.

Too Much Insensitivity

You can be standing near someone yet feel a world apart if this pattern is pulsating too strongly in your mind. You don't have to always be expressing feelings, but if you hold all of them back, intimacy is difficult to establish with someone. People could feel they have to pry out your emotions to get an idea about who you might be within you. If people perceive you as insensitive too often, they keep you at a distance. This past-life pattern may not be part of your conscious understanding. It usually lurks behind the scenes in the subconscious past-life memories. But when activated it can make expressing emotions a real challenge. If you want to bring a lover or anyone closer, this pattern will need to be brought out into the open landscape so you can gain a new understanding of how it impacts you.

Too Caring

Your sign Cancer can attract people into your life who need a great deal of attention. This past-life pattern can be traced back to previous lives in which you took being overprotective too far. If you fall into this behavior in this lifetime, it can cause others to be too dependent on you. Being emotionally supportive of those you care about is a good thing. It is when you feel responsible for someone too much of the time that your relationship can get out of balance. You can become too drained of energy if you are carrying too much of the weight in relationships. You may like being counted on by your friends, family, and lovers. When you lose sight of your boundaries is when you get into trouble.

Feelings of Insecurity

Finding a sense of security is a heartfelt need you want to maintain. If a relationship starts to eat away at your inner stability, it brings you great discomfort. Your intuition is probably sounding an alarm to remind you that this is a past-life pattern you came into this life to avoid. Your affection or feelings of attachment to someone could cause you to deny the reality of how someone is causing you mental anxiety. Your intuition may be trying to guide you away from a person who does not give you the love you badly want to receive. A refusal to see with clearer vision might keep you entangled in this pattern far longer than good for you.

Altered Perceptions: Cancer Paths to Transforming Karmic Relationship Patterns

You could experience a sigh of relief as you make your way through a karmic pattern's influence. This does often occur. It might even energize a current relationship with bold new insights. The confidence you gain in just recognizing the presence of a pattern allows you to walk along a more productive path. You could experience a feeling that the effort was well worth it to turn a past-life pattern into a sense of renewal. Relationships might seem easier to form and your ability to create greater harmony with others is possible.

Try to keep in mind if you feel a connection with a karmic pattern that you can gain a new perspective on this energy. It can seem difficult at first to get out from under the influence of a pattern if it has been with you in this life for a long time. Your steady determination to put into practice a new awareness is the key to opening the door to overcoming a pattern. Sometimes it is a retraining of our mind not to give in to the pull of a pattern's shadowy energy. The light is closer than you might think. Opening your eyes to a renewed reality starts an exciting process that will unfold into a wonderful self-discovery.

I Feel Invisible

This pattern becomes a lighter background noise when you become more assertive. If at first it is a foreign experience to act in this way, don't let it bother you. Before you know it, people will treat you with more recognition. Giving yourself permission to be self-oriented is a bold first step in pushing this past-life pattern out of the current life. Since you are one of the water signs in being a Cancer, your intuition might instinctively put a quiet space into your thought processes. This is fine, as sometimes the tranquility is your own way of sizing up situations. There is a need to step out from the serenity and take action. You will find your own goals and ideas getting support when you don't tolerate those people negating your important plans. When you put yourself first, the universe will guide you to relationships that promise fulfillment.

Mood Swings

The mood swings pattern is less problematic when you verbalize feelings. Moods in themselves are not a bad thing. Sometimes they can launch you into a new way of thinking. They can act as a barometer on how you are feeling about interactions with others. If held-back emotions build into angry moods, this pattern intensifies. It is far better to communicate with people you want to bring closer. Intimacy is easier to have with those you love when you bring your most heartfelt feelings more out in the open. When you reveal what is on your mind, the trust and even passion become a reality with the important people in your life.

Dependency-Needs Imbalance

The dependency-needs imbalance may sneak up on you when you least expect it. But with practice and consistent effort, you can turn this past-life pattern into less of a problem rather quickly. Your own self-reliance, balanced with knowing you can count on a trusted partner, keeps this pattern in check. In every relationship there will be times a person can be going through a difficult time period and needs help from a lover or friend. To keep this pattern from repeatedly entering your life, focusing on your own goals may be one way to break free. Tuning in to your own independence will empower you.

If you are in a relationship with a person who expects you to do the impossible for them on a regular basis, you will get emotionally drained. It is better for you to back off from trying to do too much. You will need to communicate what you can and cannot continually do for someone. Clearly defining your boundaries is the way to transcend this pattern.

Walking on the Moon

This pattern may require you to find techniques that keep you grounded in relating to others. Your own energy is well equipped to stay mentally and emotionally clear to avoid a spaced-out feeling. It might be good to explore meditation or yoga as a way to strengthen your inner connection to your more sensitive energy. Intuition can be a road to empowerment as you let it get expressed. There are certain individuals who, due to the chemistry they form with you, can cause you to feel off center. There may be occasions you will need to pull back to gather your own energies. Believing in the inner power you possess goes a long way to giving you the confidence to rise above this past-life influence.

Trouble Receiving

The trouble receiving pattern is best resolved by allowing yourself to receive emotional support as well as give it to others. You need to replenish your own energy by receiving. If you are constantly giving, you can feel drained of physical, mental, and emotional energy. There is a healing quality in receiving. It can give strength to your intuition as well by taking in what others are trying to give back to you. The universe wants you to balance giving and receiving. It is in this sharing that you step out of this pattern and enjoy greater relationship fulfillment.

Hermit

The hermit pattern is part of the natural Cancer inclination to want privacy. It indicates there is a need at times to seek out time alone even if you have discovered a soul mate. The key thing is to communicate to others that you find it centering to be in your own space. You probably find it easier to process the past and present when getting the private time alone. If you take the risk of including others in your ideas, it will bring them closer. This pattern does have a way of weaving a wall of seclusion around you if you fear letting others into your life. If you find the courage to take small steps to venture out, you allow the universe to bring the people you need for happiness into your life. If you have faith in your intuition, it will guide you to form relationships with individuals who respect your need for privacy and enjoy the time shared together.

Digging Up the Seed

The way out of this past-life pattern is to stick around in a relationship at the first signs of adversity. Sometimes it is in facing the problems that the deeper harmony breaks through. It takes time for a relationship to truly reveal itself. Focusing more on the positives to being with a person than the negatives often opens the door to clearer communication. Don't feel bad if you prefer short-term relationships. But if you are desiring a long-term commitment, believing you have much to offer could be the key to making this happen. Accepting the fact there are no perfect people takes some of the intensity out of this pattern. Patience is an important part of gaining clarity and finding the relationship fulfillment you wish to attain.

If it is more that this pattern appears in the form of other people in your life, it gives you an opportunity to perceive this. If you want to stay in relationships with those who have adopted this pattern, it can be disappointing. The main thing is that you are not denying what you see. You will be closer to finding the right person for you when identifying this pattern manifesting through someone else. It is the universe showing you that this is a pattern you don't want to accept.

Territorial Tension

When you make your goals and priorities clear to others, there is less of a chance the territorial tension pattern will prevail. At least you will have staked your claim to your own turf in a relationship. Your own empowerment and passion come forward faster when you assertively walk your talk. To keep this pattern from repeating in this incarnation you may need to make some compromises. Your intuition finds strength when you feel inner stability. Your relationships benefit greatly when you know your own personal power is respected. A feeling of independence keeps this pattern away from you and points the way to creating relationship harmony.

Past Fears

The past fears pattern takes some practice in not superimposing experiences from the past onto new relationship encounters. This pattern can suddenly emerge in a current relationship that has been going on for a while. It helps to begin to realize negative memories have no power over you. You need to replace them with as many positive images in your mind as possible. It does take some work to release a past-life memory to keep it from interfering with the happiness you want to have in your life. Finding success in one wholesome relationship can heal all those past memories. You might be surprised at how fast this process can take place.

Too Much Insensitivity

To keep this pattern out of your relationships, all you need to do is make a more conscious effort to express feelings. The water element that colors the sign Cancer can influence you to be cautious about sharing your inner world. Showing you care about someone through your words and actions is a bold first step beyond the border of this pattern. If for whatever reason you are not comfortable with the emotional side of life, you don't need to always say how you feel. When you are a good listener, you prove to others you are really there for them. Taking the risk occasionally to speak what you are feeling opens the door to greater intimacy, passion, and the fulfillment you long to have.

Too Caring

The too caring pattern only becomes a reality if you try to do too much for others. There is a natural drive as a Cancer to be very loyal to those you care about. Reaching out to support those people you are close to is important to you. There are times when allowing a partner to find their own footing in dealing with a problem empowers them. It is a delicate balance to know when to take a hands-on or hands-off approach in letting someone take responsibility for a decision. With practice you can get good at doing this. Your emotional and mental energy stays clearer and stronger to help people when you keep a clear sense of boundaries.

Feelings of Insecurity

The feelings of insecurity pattern need not interfere with your relationship happiness. A Cancer Sun sign person like yourself is a fish out of water when not feeling internally stable in relationships. To support your sense of identity and creative passion in your soul, you need to know people respect your need for emotional peace. When you aren't afraid to go through adversity with a partner, the relationship gains strength. Each time the two of you face problems together, you secure your trust for each other. You keep this past-life pattern from interfering with your relationship fulfillment by letting your intuition guide you to individuals who value peace of mind as much as you do.

The Cancer Reward from Solving Karmic Patterns

When you first realize a karmic pattern has followed you into this life, it is an opportunity to overcome the influence. Don't judge yourself as having been doing something wrong, but rather celebrate in gaining new insight. Your Cancer intuition and mental power have found a new ally in tuning in to the confidence to put a pattern to rest. It is a journey to take those first steps in rising above a past-life pattern. You will sense a renewed energy in getting a broader perspective about past-life energies. What was once a shadowy force possibly causing self-doubt becomes a beacon of light shining rays of a new bold confidence upon you.

It does take putting new understanding into practice to keep a pattern at a distance. You could be surprised at how fast you can integrate your comprehension of past-life energies in a positive way into the current incarnation. Don't get discouraged if you take a step back when trying to walk past the hold of a pattern. Keep a positive attitude and you will achieve the growth you desire.

Stay patient and the path forward is easier to attain. Inner clarity and relationship harmony are wonderful rewards in transcending past-life patterns. Fulfilling relationship experiences will greet you when you gain new perceptions as you face the challenge represented by a past-life pattern.

FIVE
LEO: THE LEADER

Dates: July 22 to August 21

Element: Fire

Strengths: Willpower, creative ingenuity, promoting skills

Challenges: Fixed ideas, loss of confidence, controlling

Karmic Relationship Primary Shadow: Fear of failure

Key to Transforming Karmic Patterns: Being open to change

The Leo Current-Life
Relationship Landscape

If you were born under the sign of Leo, you want the world to take notice of you. When confident, your personality often opens up new adventures in meeting people. You enjoy individuals who know how to celebrate life. Those who aren't afraid to share their goals and ideas openly attract your attention. There are times you are quieter when it comes to letting others know your most heartfelt dreams. People who like to laugh and yet have serious plans pique your interest. The traditional slogan in astrology for your sign is "I create." People who naturally have a creative drive stimulate your mind.

Leo has an underlying sensitivity that might get revealed to someone when you spend time with them. You are at your best when inspiring others to act with confidence. You can be a cheerleader who wins the hearts of your closest companions. It is that look in your eyes that says you really care about a person that keeps them close.

Paying attention to the needs of someone ignites the passion and intimacy when you are together. Independent individuals intrigue you. You are at your best when encouraging others to explore their own goals, but you don't necessarily want them to wander too far ahead without you.

People who support your own goals win your loyalty. Your pride to be strong sometimes needs strokes of attention. You can be a loner but soon miss the touch and feel of a loved one. When you show your love and affection with no motives, the universe rewards you with abundance and the love you need.

The Leo Past-Life Karmic Relationship Patterns

Past-life memories have followed everyone into this lifetime. Each of us has certain past patterns that can get activated in the current incarnation. If one or more of the patterns being discussed seems familiar, don't let it bother you. Just think of it as leftover homework from previous lives needing to be completed. Go at your own pace. This is no competition like in a racing event. In dealing with a pattern you are embarking on a journey of self-discovery. Think of it as the universe trying to get you to alter a behavior to let more fulfilling experiences unfold.

As a Leo, your ability to state an intended goal and reach it is always within your grasp. Karmic patterns need not stand in the way of finding harmony with special people. Don't worry if you seem to be repeating a behavior. With that lionlike roar from the depth of your sign, there is no past-life influence that cannot be resolved. It will make your steps lighter and your path to relationship happiness easier to attain when you begin to tune in to a past-life pattern. With regular effort, it will be possible to channel the energy of a past pattern into creative directions.

Center Stage Is Always Mine

The sign Leo has a natural impulse to attract attention. If this urge gets out of control, it brings this pattern into your life. Sharing the stage in your everyday life makes others feel valued. If someone begins to get the feeling their own goals are getting too dominated by your own aspirations, resentment can become a reality. If this past-life pattern is too big a part of your everyday life people lose trust you will support their own most important goals. Sometimes a pattern like this one is not in the awareness of the conscious mind. It is hidden in our subconscious and interferes with the harmony with others we would like to have.

Another way this pattern appears is if you are attracting individuals into your life who wear this behavior. The universe could be offering you an opportunity to observe the behavior in others so that you might realize this is a past-life pattern you want to avoid. In other words, it is your own potential pattern, but before embracing it, you can gain the insight to not enter into it.

Lack of Ego Strength

Leo is known to be a strong lion. In some past lives that inner fortitude lost its way and was too diluted. Your self-confidence became too negated from the input of others. This past-life pattern might be getting in the way of your creative thinking. Your movement forward to pursue meaningful relationships can get impacted as well. You may not feel deserving of a wonderful soul mate. This is a pattern that can find you backing off from forming a commitment with someone who could be the right person for you. You could be blocking the positive support people are trying to offer you. A Leo like you feels like something is badly missing without a natural heartbeat of self-assurance.

Too Much Pride

A fear of failure can be the root cause of this pattern. Being proud of yourself is a good thing, as it often ignites inspiring goals. If activated, this past-life pattern can get you to think a relationship will not succeed due to self-doubt. If you hide this way of thinking, it will cause confusion within your own thinking and in that of others. People will become alienated if you sit on fear of failure for long time periods. This pattern will at times make it difficult for you to let others tune in to your emotional nature. You will be perceived as having a wall around you, making it hard for others to enter. True communication becomes a tall order to attain. Often at the root of this past-life pattern is a negative outlook that may be blocking the fulfillment you can have. A refusal to talk about the issues you are hiding results in great distance between you and others. A fear of showing any vulnerability is another indication this past-life influence has made an appearance.

Compulsive Need for Love

If this pattern followed you into this incarnation, it is a driving force to keep confirming you need love. The problem with this is when you are never satisfied with any relationship. It can be caused by more than one reason. One is low self-esteem. In this instance it doesn't matter who you are with in this pattern. You do not feel deserving of the relationship. It does not mean in all of your past lives this was a problem. It is only in those lives where this type of thinking grew too strong. It kept you then and possibly now moving impulsively from one relationship to another without much clear thinking. Another offshoot of this past-life influence was searching for that perfect person. It became an endless frustration to satisfy an impossible quest. You were never really happy in that you could not accept others the way they were. Your life too often lacked stability. If this pattern visits you too often in current life, a feeling of discontent is too much a reality.

Moving Too Impulsively Fast

You are a Leo fire sign who can get moving spontaneously in the fast lane. If you find yourself too impatient with people, there is a good possibility this tendency is a past-life carryover. This could appear to others like you are too easily distracted from paying attention to them. People will feel you are not present even while in the same room. Listening and real communication are not as vibrant as they need to be. Closeness and intimacy become too absent with those you want to keep near you. Your own life goals begin to drown out those of lovers and friends. Not making time for important people causes them to drift away. Losing sight of supporting the goals of others weakens their trust if this pattern is a regular visitor.

Too Tight-Lipped

Leo is known as being dramatic and at times outspoken. If you are very quiet when your feelings are hurt and have a tendency to hide your emotions, this behavior could be linked to this past-life pattern. There are times you may want to process your thoughts before reacting to situations. If you are in the habit of not stating your ideas more directly, it can confuse others. This occurs for different reasons. One may be that in some past lives your opinions were discounted and even ignored. It could be that this painful recollection resides in your memory. It is causing you to fall back into this behavior. Another possibility for this past-life pattern to manifest is due to not trusting someone. You go on the defensive by not revealing how you really feel when asked for some input of your own ideas. If you stay attached to this pattern, your closeness with others becomes turned into distance.

Hurt Ego

Your persona that you show the world may be a mask to conceal a very sensitive side of you. Criticism may be something that sends your mind into a tailspin. This is a past-life pattern that can find you overreacting to circumstances that might surprise people you are close to. You might wonder why very suddenly you allow some people to rub you the wrong way. This pattern can bring out angry outbursts that can give you a sense of losing control. You are a card-carrying Leo, which means you have natural instincts to maintain a solid stabilizing life. This pattern reveals an inner world that you came into this life to heal. It shows that in some past lives perhaps you took in more criticism than you could handle. Certain people or situations will act as a trigger, igniting this pattern and sometimes causing you to act in ways you later wish you had not.

Ignoring Your Limits

A fire sign like yourself might be tempted to take unnecessary risks. This is a past-life pattern that could find you boldly entering relationships not in your best interest. You could be partnering with people more focused on their own goals and ignoring your own. The equality you are hoping for is tilted too far toward others. This begins to take away from your happiness in a big way. You may have been attracted to someone at first sight who looked like the right match for you. If you deny the reality that your needs are not being met, you may stay in these types of relationships far too long. That Leo courage to explore the unknown and seek new adventure needs to be directed to a relationship that promises greater fulfillment. The problem this past-life pattern can present is that it plays on your drive to maintain a relationship even if it is not what it had promised to be.

Fixed Opinions

You have great persistence to follow through on plans you want to achieve. If this past-life pattern finds its way into your life, a tendency to hold on to your own viewpoints may cause you to clash with others. When flexibility is missing too frequently, people can react with anger. You can appear like an immovable force. Those you love will distance themselves if you continue to act in this way. Sometimes this pattern appears when you feel a need to stay in control of the outcome of decisions with people. It is what looks like your lack of openness to alternative ideas that can cause tension in communicating with others. If you fail to listen to opposing views or suggestions as a regular event, you do not get the cooperation you want. Compromise is too much a foreign word in your mind.

Bullying

Promoting your ideas comes naturally for you as a Leo. It is when you are forcing your plans on others to get your own way that this past-life pattern intensifies. It doesn't mean in past incarnations you always demonstrated this behavior. It could even be that this memory is linked to particular lives in which you were too overpowered by others and it is triggering an overactive use of this tendency. If you get too pushy, you will bring others to react angrily. The main effect of this pattern is that it keeps the harmony and greater love you hope to achieve with someone from happening. The realization that you can get more of what you need through trusting your closest companions is missing. Exhibiting bullying behavior keeps the closeness with others at a distance.

Trying Too Hard to Impress

This pattern implies that in some past lives you went out of your way to impress others as a way to be liked. Riding this pattern to extremes takes you away from forming genuine connections with others. There is nothing wrong with wanting to be perceived favorably. It is giving an exaggerated portrayal of yourself that can cause confusion when wanting to establish an intimate relationship. Everyone has an outward personality they show the world. If becoming too regularly used, this pattern gets in between you and those you are trying to bring close. It presents a challenge to others to break through what feels and looks like a wall concealing the real you.

Angry Moods

Letting anger build is a path backtracking into this past-life pattern. It is when holding back your feelings that the anger starts to become war clouds. You may be launching into angry outbursts over circumstances totally unrelated to how the anger started in the first place. Rather than you being in the moment with how you feel, this pattern entices you into holding back your emotional intensity. Sooner or later that stuffed anger comes firing out. You are a fire sign that does better when you are open about your ideas and insights. There is a good chance those who know you the best will sense there is something bothering you. When your timing is off in expressing anger, it creates disruption and tension in your relationships.

Altered Perceptions: Leo Paths to Transforming Karmic Relationship Patterns

You will feel like you have more energy and a brighter outlook on life when releasing a karmic pattern from your mind. The world seems full of more opportunities when letting go of a past-life shadowy energy. The balance and harmony in relationships seem to magically be easier to attain. Attracting compatible partners has an easier flow. Your insights into what you need in a relationship might become clearer.

If any of the karmic patterns discussed hit a nerve in you, don't let it bother you. The important thing is identifying if a pattern of behavior is interfering with your ability to enjoy fulfillment in your relating to others. This is the first step to gaining the clarity to turn the energy into a more productive expression. You may be surprised by your own ability to transcend a past-life pattern through just becoming more aware of the tendency to repeat a pattern. A new path of self-discovery unfolds when you gain a new perception and attitude in learning how to let go of a pattern. Your mental, physical, and intuitive energies gain strength when you no longer allow a past-life pattern to be a reality.

Center Stage Is Always Mine

When you share the power in a relationship, this pattern will disappear as though it was never there. By empowering others, you bring a sense of wholesome equality into your relationships. People will know you value them and you will be developing a great mutual support system. If this is a very ingrained pattern, it won't change overnight. But with some consistent practice you will begin to see sooner if you are stepping too far into someone's space. Your sign Leo needs a great deal of personal freedom. That elbow room you require is needed by your friends, family members, and lovers as well.

If you are inviting people into your life who do not respect your own territory, think of it as an opportunity to recognize this as perhaps a past-life pattern that was once a big part of you. This is your chance to realize you don't need to go back into playing out this role again. You likely will find that someone lost in this pattern is not the right person to keep in your everyday life.

Lack of Ego Strength

If this pattern is shadowing you in this incarnation, it symbolizes that you need to embody a bolder expression of yourself. The good news is that when manifesting the colors of the fiery sign Leo, you can tune in to the assertiveness you require. Walking and talking with confidence strengthens your identity and makes you more likely to land in relationships that bring harmony. It keeps away people who drown out your own self-expression when you project a belief in yourself. You were born under a sign that wants you to make your presence very visible. This is the road map to raising your relationships to the level of fulfillment you prefer.

Too Much Pride

The too much pride pattern can be channeled into a new direction by a willingness to let down your guard. You have more inner strength than you may realize at times. Your sign Leo sometimes gets empowered when you respond to a challenge. The competitive power in you only needs to get focused in a new direction to turn the negative energy in this pattern into a winning formula for yourself. Letting others know that you are having trouble communicating when you feel emotionally bottled up can open the door to a deeper intimacy. Nobody expects you to always be a tower of strength. You find a sense of renewal by surrendering your fear of becoming vulnerable. What might have appeared to your mind as a weakness becomes a new source of strength in expressing honest communication.

Compulsive Need for Love

The compulsive need for love pattern can be overcome through coming to the realization that you deserve a fulfilling relationship. Developing a positive mindset goes far in keeping this past-life pattern away from you. This pattern requires your patience, as it might take some time to move in a new direction. You may not find a perfect partner, but you can be successful in being with a compatible person. The key thing to remember is that maintaining a new perspective in what will bring harmonious relationships into your life is important. In some ways this takes retraining your mind to find people who appreciate your ideas and who want an equal partnership. The compulsiveness to run to new relationships lessens as you grow comfortable with wanting stability.

Moving Too Impulsively Fast

This pattern is not that difficult to convert into a more productive winning expression. It is amazing how when you show you are listening to the important people in your life, it makes love and friendship more vibrant. It is okay as a Leo to passionately pursue your own goals. If you slow down long enough to include others in big decisions, it makes them feel valued. You are a fire sign, so moving quickly comes naturally. Just remember not to lose sight of those you care about along your life journey. Clear communication gives a greater depth to your relationships and attracts the support you will always appreciate.

Too Tight-Lipped

The too tight-lipped pattern probably sounds counterintuitive for the sign Leo. Your sign will often push you to be direct. The closer you are to someone in your life, the higher chance a past-life tendency might intervene, finding you holding back feelings. When you take the risk of revealing your emotional side, there is a greater chance to have the intimacy you desire. Sometimes it is that first leap of faith to boldly let your ideas be known when this pattern begins to recede. With some practice in communicating more openly, you may be surprised how it becomes a regular occurrence and the pattern might seem like it never existed. Letting those you want to keep close into your inner world makes the relationships stronger. When you trust that it is okay to speak your heartfelt thoughts, you take on a path to greater harmony in your relating to others.

Hurt Ego

If activated, the hurt ego pattern could be bringing up painful memories of when you endured great opposition to your dreams. Leo is known for shaking off criticism and passionately pursuing life goals with a fiery spirit. There is a talent in compartmentalizing a problem to keep it from interfering with your life. If you can come to a realization that current relationship encounters may be bringing back past-life memories, you will begin to overcome this pattern. You might be able to trace back your overreaction to people challenging your ideas. Learning to take a cool-down period to gain greater objectivity may help you gain the insight to get clarity about this past-life pattern. It could take some time to transcend emotional bruises from past incarnations. Your patience in facing this pattern will pay great dividends along your life journey.

If you are in a relationship with someone overly critical in unreasonable ways, this pattern will likely keep resurfacing. It will require you to steer clear of people negating your every move in order for you to let go of this pattern. You don't need to search for perfect people. The main point here is discriminating which individuals want a similar path to harmony.

Ignoring Your Limits

This pattern only needs you to take a reality check to make sure you did not rush into a relationship that looked promising but is not really in your best interest. If you stop denying this is what you bargained for, you will be freer to move on to a more fulfilling relationship. It might take courage to move past someone who does not support your hopes and dreams. The Leo strength you possess could at times find you with overconfidence that you can change the person you are involved with in a relationship into something they are not willing to be. When you come to the realization you have given a person every chance to change their behavior with no results, the path to finding better options begins with this new awakened perception. Moving forward will feel like a refreshing breath of air and allow you to create relationships that give you as much as you are giving to someone else.

Fixed Opinions

The fixed opinions pattern is not so hard to budge out of your way. Showing some degree of flexibility goes far in taking away the likelihood this pattern will come between you and someone else. As a Leo, you can display that rugged determination to make your goals come true. There will be times your plans will conflict with the people closest to you. If you adopt a win-win strategy, it brings others to support your needs because you are showing you want to do the same for them. You don't need to sacrifice your own dreams to please anyone. If you show you are not oppositional to change and can adapt to new situations, your relationships do flow better. You actually get empowered through sharing your power.

Bullying

The bullying pattern is masking feelings of insecurity. Releasing a need to overpower others opens the door to new rewarding relationships. People will want to come closer. Trusting that you don't need to force your ideas on others is the first step out of this past-life shadow. Your own goals will get the support you need when you realize there is no need to manipulate people into your way of thinking. Through learning to trust your closest companions, you will make falling into this pattern less likely. When you walk away from a tendency to use this type of behavior, the fulfilling relationships you need are more likely to happen. By releasing the hold of this pattern, the universe responds with offering you alternative perceptions to attract the harmony in others you long to find.

Trying Too Hard to Impress

The trying too hard to impress pattern need not remain as part of your way of relating to individuals. When you reveal more of your natural thinking, people lock on to a faster clarity about you. This could be linked to certain past incarnations in which you were not readily accepted for just being you. Coming out of the shadow of this pattern's influence only needs you to have more faith in yourself. It might not happen in one day, but the more you practice not pretending to be someone you are not, the closer you are to finding fulfilling relationships. Small steps in a new direction will lead to eventually taking bigger ones. If you find the right people to have in your life, you don't need to act out a role that is not you. Revealing your authentic self wins the trust of individuals you want in your life.

Angry Moods

The angry moods pattern need not be feared. Anger is an emotion that will leak out no matter how much any of us tries to hide it. You are better off letting out some steam rather than letting hidden intense feelings snowball out of control. There are times anger clears the air in relationships. If it is not used to manipulate or coerce, you will find this pattern not so prevalent in your life. Forgiveness is a great ally if anger comes between you and someone. Holding long grudges only serves to distance you from people. Learning to communicate your thoughts when feeling heated up over a situation might keep a problem from escalating. There are instances when a cooling down period is wise as long as you do come back and try to work out an issue with someone. The key thing to remember is waiting too long and sitting on anger has a tendency to make your perceptions get unclear. There is much truth in dealing with a problem sooner rather than later to keep the peace with those you love.

The Leo Reward from Solving Karmic Patterns

Your Leo persistence to respond to the challenge of a karmic pattern paves the way for new insights. Once you have new eyes to see through a past-life pattern, there is a great chance you will stay vigilant in not repeating a past pattern. The Leo passion that colors your fiery spirit will rejoice in channeling a shadowy energy into positive directions. The personal empowerment in your footsteps will make your relationships ring with greater harmony.

Don't let it worry you if one or more of the past-life patterns discussed has been too much a part of your life journey. It is in gaining new insight into a past-life pattern that bold new perceptions give you more opportunities to enjoy all your relationships.

If you accept a need to be more flexible and accept change, it makes it easier to overcome past-life patterns. They have no real power over you. By stepping out of their influence through a new attitude of self-discovery, you could be surprised how the universe makes it possible to discover the joy you want to experience with the people you already know and the ones you are yet to meet.

SIX
VIRGO: THE PERFECTIONIST

Dates: August 22 to September 21

Element: Earth

Strengths: Organizing, dedication to learning new skills, thorough thinking

Challenges: Narrow outlook, self-doubt, unrealistic standards of perfection

Karmic Relationship Primary Shadow: Too attached to a limiting vision

Key to Transforming Karmic Patterns: A new empowering belief system

The Virgo Current-Life Relationship Landscape

If you were born under the sign Virgo, you are blessed with the power of a strong analytical mind. Your closest friends and lovers probably depend on your problem-solving ability. Your attention to detail is the envy of the other signs in that you see things others may miss. The traditional astrology phrase for Virgo is "I organize." You can be supportive of those people you care about in unique ways, winning their loyalty.

You enjoy people letting you be yourself. If someone puts you under a microscope, you wish they would cut you some slack. You can tolerate some criticism, but if it becomes extreme, you tend to tune this out of your mind. When you offer advice and know when to stop giving it, people are open to your suggestions.

You trust those who communicate without hidden agendas. It is then you will do the same for them. You find that people love you more when you don't demand too much perfection from them. If someone becomes too emotionally dependent, you will do your best to comfort them. You will look for them to return a shoulder to lean on when you need one.

A lover who does not pressure you to open up your feeling side too fast will win your heart. The inner strength you possess attracts someone who recognizes it. You tend to hide your emotions until a person proves he or she is worthy to have them shown to them.

Some individuals will perceive you as complicated. You see yourself as having your own way of processing life through a carefully organized mental filter. The more a person gets to know your thought processes the closer they can be to you. Falling in love for you may begin with a few small steps that eventually become a run. When you believe in the potential for a relationship to thrive, you are willing to become a solid and committed partner.

The Virgo Past-Life Karmic Relationship Patterns

Each of us comes into an incarnation with past-life memories. You probably will not find each of the karmic past-life patterns discussed as part of your own reality. If one or more seem like part of your way of living in the world, don't get too worried. The information in this book is meant to be a guide to bring greater awareness. You could find a path to empowerment in dealing with a past-life pattern.

As a Virgo, your laser-like perceptions may only need a gentle tweak in a new direction to rise above a past-life pattern. It takes patience to put new learning into practice. There is no need to judge yourself. There is no race against time to come a new understanding of how to better express the energy in past-life patterns. A sense of renewed energy and greater joy is possible in getting a clearer view of a past pattern.

Too Picky

Your sign Virgo gives you a natural tendency to scrutinize carefully which individuals you want as close friends or lovers. It is possible a past-life instinct followed you into this incarnation to look for perfection that is impossible to find in a person. If you raise the bar to extreme heights, people will have trouble meeting you halfway in a relationship. This past-life pattern can be a defense mechanism to keep people at a distance. Just be sure you aren't too finely sifting in what you think you perceive in someone. It might be that your wonderful ability to analyze is seeing imperfections in a person. This could cause you to miss out on a good relationship.

Another way this pattern could come your way is through a person expecting too much perfection from you. The universe may be showing you the pattern of behavior in someone else to allow you to realize you don't want to repeat this pattern yourself.

Rush to Judgment

This is a past-life pattern that will find you doubting the future success of a relationship very fast. This could be a repeating theme in this incarnation that is still an active part of your thought processes. Not giving enough time to develop a relationship with someone might be linked to this pattern. The usual patience of an earth sign like yourself is missing. There are times your intuition will quickly signal a person is not right for you. That is good in that you have made a decision to move away from people who would not be positive influences. But if you never really wait long enough to let the depth of a relationship reveal itself, you are likely missing out on a good partnership.

Loss of Hope

This pattern is connected to some past lives where you had self-esteem problems. It impacted your hope to find a suitable relationship. You did not feel worthy of receiving love and affection. A negative outlook sometimes attracted the wrong type of partner. If this pattern gets activated in the current incarnation, it can cause you to try to fit into relationships lacking harmony. You are denying yourself the chance to choose people with a greater possibility of working toward a happier reality. You likely will be working too hard to keep a relationship afloat if you are too engaged in this pattern.

Mind in the Rearview Mirror

There are times you could feel like you have been snagged in the clutches of this past-life pattern if you remain fixated on a relationship that did not work. You may be comparing new love interests you meet to a past lover and holding them to unrealistic expectations. It could be that in some past incarnations when you suffered a hurtful disappointment in a relationship, it prevented you from moving on to a new one. This memory could have come alive again and is blocking your ability to open up your feelings to a new person. It could even be causing tension in an existing relationship if the pattern intensifies. If you are unwilling to let go of a past romance that has no chance to come back, it makes it difficult to enjoy the promise of a new partner. There is the possibility you are denying what went wrong in a relationship that has ended. You are only remembering the good from the past encounter and refusing to examine what the issues were.

Too Much Anxiety

If you are extremely worried about whether or not you are perfect enough to be in a relationship, you could be playing off a script written by this past-life pattern. The perceptive eye you have for detail can turn inward, causing you too much anxiety to commit to a relationship. Virgo is ruled by the planet Mercury, that winged messenger of the gods in Greek mythology. Sometimes your mind may be flying too much in worrying about making mistakes by being with someone. It makes it a real challenge to trust people if you are in the habit of questioning if you have the right stuff to be in a relationship. You could be with a very compatible person, but your mental anxiety is bringing a lack of stability into the relationship. The tendency to pull back due to feeling uncomfortable with others is a clue this past-life pattern is too prevalent in your life.

Stuck in Routine Thinking

This past-life pattern may appear in the form of holding on to your own territory in uncompromising ways. Adapting to the needs of others is not easy if you are fixated on your own routines. Communication is a challenge if you are afraid to leave your comfort zones. You may have great expectations for others to do most of the adjusting in the relationship. Power struggles result on a regular basis if you are too attached to this past pattern of thought. Harmony and intimacy will likely seem like strangers. There is an underlying theme of wanting to stay in control. Holding on to old ways of thinking without listening to the ideas of others makes a meeting of the minds difficult.

The Critic

You can be very aware of how the actions and words of individuals impact your everyday living. There are times you may wish that natural radar you possess to analyze the habits of others was turned off. Occasionally criticizing the people you are closest with likely is not going to be a problem. If you can't stop being a critic, a great deal of tension manifests. If this past-life pattern kicks in strongly, all you see is what you don't like. You might not realize you are forgetting to accent the positive when someone does something you approve of. That Virgo attention to detail can accomplish great things. It is putting someone you care about too much under a microscope that can get them to react angrily and cause them to pull away.

There is another way this pattern can present itself. It may be a partner or friend who displays this pattern. It may be that you have come into this incarnation to drop this behavior and are being presented a direct viewing coming from someone else. It is your chance to perceive this as a pattern you don't want to embrace for yourself.

Surrendered Identity

There is a service-oriented instinct in your sign, Virgo. Others feel at ease when you are supportive of their most important goals. If carried over from a past-life, your identity is clouded by trying too hard to make the lives of others a success. Your own plans for the future may get lost in trying to please other individuals. Your assertiveness becomes watered down by not speaking up for your own ideas if this pattern becomes a reality. Your own personal empowerment is being submerged under the thinking you must feed into the power of someone else. The equality in a relationship is missing, keeping you in a subservient role.

Extreme Worrying

If this past-life pattern is a frequent visitor, it can get you to overthink how you relate to people. You are expecting too much perfection from yourself in unrealistic ways. If pointed inward, that great power to analyze is an obsessive tendency that can get you into too much negative thinking. You can be trying to please everyone all the time. Being afraid to make a mistake is often at the root system of this pattern lurking in past-life memories. A fear of stepping out of this pattern keeps you trapped in it. The fulfillment you are in search of in a relationship stays out of your reach until you walk away from this shadowy energy.

I Am Not Deserving

Giving out love and affection but not being comfortable with receiving them from others is an indication this past-life pattern has some sway over you. It could be you don't feel worthy of a fulfilling relationship. It is possible you are in a good, rewarding romance or friendship but still resist accepting the fact you deserve love. Some past lives that lacked the emotional warmth you wanted may be interfering with your ability to trust the love coming your way in this incarnation. Those people closest to you may sense you tighten up when they try to reward you with positive support and compliments. Finding your way to accept the intimacy and love you deserve in this life is the challenge.

Denying Anger

A clue this past-life pattern has emerged into your current incarnation is if you are too timid in expressing anger. This will likely create some intense moods you don't want to feel. Your perceptions about people may become clouded by an inner emotional intensity due to bottled up anger. Rather than deal with a tense situation in the present, you will be drained of energy by carrying around hurt feelings. There is some truth that taking some downtime before overreacting to a situation might be wise. But if you are repeatedly hiding your opposition to someone's behavior, eventually you could explode more than you wanted to. It is very possible that in some past lives you dealt with anger by not expressing it for fear of someone's reaction. Your memory of these lives could be influencing your thinking in this life.

Ruled by Guilt

This past-life pattern is a reenactment from incarnations that found you feeling too responsible for the problems of others. You were blamed too much of the time for mistakes being made by other people. In this life you could become the scapegoat again if you give in to guilt. Taking on too much responsibility to bail people out of trouble they created begins to wear you out. The harmony you long for is being swallowed up by losing sight of your boundaries.

Another way this past-life pattern exposes itself is through individuals who know how to push your guilt buttons. They are manipulating you into a guilt trip. It is an opportunity to say no, you can't go back into a pattern you came into this incarnation to avoid. If you deny that you are doing favors for others out of guilt, this past-life influence will ensnare you.

Altered Perceptions: Virgo Paths to Transforming Karmic Relationship Patterns

Your mind will feel like it has been given a wonderful recharge when gaining clarity about a past-life pattern. It may even feel like the shadow force of a karmic pattern never really had any control over you. The harmony you want to enjoy in your relationships will seem much easier to attain. It is an empowering feeling to escape the hold of a pattern of behavior that was interfering with your happiness.

There is nothing to fear if any of the past-life patterns that will be discussed sounds very familiar. The main thing to remember is that in acknowledging a pattern you can begin to move in a new direction. Taking what was a limiting or negative energy into a more positive expression is liberating. The insight you gain in facing a past-life energy can give you enlightened eyes to find the fulfillment you

seek in relationships and other areas of your life. It is a learning process that takes some practice to move past any karmic pattern. There
is no need to judge yourself if you identify with any of the patterns
discussed. The key thing to remember is that taking those initial steps
to bring a past-life pattern into clearer focus can allow you the love
you hope to experience.

Too Picky

If the too picky past-life pattern seems like too big a part of your
perceptions of people, it might be a lingering energy from past
incarnations. You need to have as a mantra that there are no perfect
people. What you are viewing as imperfection in someone could
be their uniqueness. Letting yourself go beyond your comfort zone
allows you to interact with individuals who may be a good match
for you. Sometimes it is being open to differences in one another
that makes a relationship stimulating. You could need to accept a
person the way they are, the same way you hope to be embraced by
them. There is nothing wrong with being careful about who you
allow to get to know you in an intimate way. But if you are too
narrow about the type of person you think you need to be happy,
it does limit your options. The happiness and harmony you want
in a relationship are closer than you think. It may only take alter-
ing your expectations slightly to bring into reality a very fulfilling
partnership.

Rush to Judgment

There is an inner restless energy that can manifest in the rush to
judgment pattern. If this past-life shadow force is too prevalent in
your current life, there is a tendency to move impatiently away from
relationships. Taking the time to get to really know someone may

prove rewarding. Steering away from jumping to conclusions about people lessens the intensity of this past-life pattern. If you slow down, you could enjoy having a person in your life who supports your goals and is there for you during a challenging time period. The hold of this pattern is less likely if you realize the potential for a relationship to be fulfilling needs time to develop. If you grow comfortable in patiently communicating your needs to someone, you can find your way out of this pattern's influence.

Loss of Hope

In this pattern you have to put yourself first even if it feels strange to do so. You will find it brings this past-life energy into balance. The tendency to serve others is in the DNA of the sign Virgo. People in some past lives likely took advantage of your generosity. You came into this life to make sure you did not go overboard in pleasing others. In making sure your own identity and goals are being supported by people you are close to, you will find your relationships walking down harmony lane. It will be faster than you might think to overcome this pattern if you remember to check in with yourself to make sure you are being recognized as an equal.

Mind in the Rearview Mirror

This pattern does take retraining your mind to look forward rather than back to the past. Letting go of a past relationship from this lifetime or a previous incarnation allows the possibility of being with someone who meets the needs of who you are in the present. Weaning yourself away from the memory of the person, who you thought was someone you can't live without, slowly releases a new revitalized energy in you. In releasing the past, the universe often responds with a magical synchronicity to bring us new individuals in our life with a similar desire for a fulfilling relationship. Keeping your focus on the here and now awakens the future with more rewarding options.

Too Much Anxiety

The too much anxiety pattern can be overcome through staying away from unnecessary worry about what you can't control. There is a wonderful ability in Virgo to be a careful planner. Sometimes a relationship gets messy because nobody is perfect. If you let go of the fear of making mistakes in a relationship, you will be happier and find a greater level of comfort in being with someone. You may find that your closest friends and loved ones don't expect the impossible from you. Taking the pressure of unrealistic expectations off yourself paves the way for happiness and fulfillment. Having a regular routine that channels nervous energy away from you could relax your mind to keep away the tendency to over worry.

Stuck in Routine Thinking

This pattern can be conquered by being open to new ideas. It often is comforting for a Virgo like yourself to stick to what works for you. Being flexible helps you maintain harmony in your relationships. There is a capacity to adapt to change in your sign. When you make use of this ability, people are more likely to be supportive of your important goals. Being willing to step out of your comfort zones does keep this pattern in check. The love and fulfillment come to you faster when you let go of a need to keep life too predictable. You give the universe an opportunity to surprise you with rewarding relationships when you aren't too resistant to new perceptions.

The Critic

The critic pattern only needs you to point the awareness you have toward a positive direction. You may find it easier than you think to convert this past-life influence into a more favorable experience. If you focus on what someone is doing right in your opinion, they may begin to change a behavior you find annoying. Positive support given to those people you care about is a sure path to creating harmony. Being a Virgo adorns you with valuable insights into the minds of others. Working harder on the issues rather than trying to change someone is a bridge to greater fulfillment with that person.

It can also be true that you don't have to accept being a regular target of criticism. If you regularly attract individuals into your life who act out this pattern, then the universe is trying to make you aware that this is not an energy you want to adopt. Sometimes a past-life pattern we once were in the habit of using comes to us through someone else. It is a chance to be vigilant to guard against accepting this as part of your own thought processes.

Surrendered Identity

The surrendered identity pattern is balanced by remembering to nourish the goals that inspire your mind and soul. It truly is the way beyond the reach of this pattern if it should try to influence you. Virgo is an earth sign, which means you need to stay grounded to your own unique path. It is from here you have much to offer without losing yourself in the life of someone else. Love is a wonderful thing that you enjoy more when being true to your own needs. It is easier to be there for people you care about when you are tuned in to your own identity. Your intuition, mind, and emotions function from a very high level when you express yourself from a clear connection to your identity. Others benefit when they show a recognition of your own unique gifts.

Extreme Worrying

The extreme worrying past-life pattern has a pathway from which to escape. The challenge is finding it. One of the keys to the trail leading away from this past-life influence is not being afraid to make mistakes. There are no perfect people or relationships. You probably need to take the pressure of unrealistic expectations off of you. This will take great tension out of your relating to others. The intimacy you hope to experience is easier to accomplish when you don't try to be too perfect. You will more comfortably adjust to a relationship when you are not preoccupied with trying to do everything just right. It might take some practice for not worrying to become a natural component of how you engage in a relationship, but it is well worth the effort.

I Am Not Deserving

This pattern is asking you to change your attitude about receiving compliments and affection. It gives a smoother flow to your sharing in relationships when you are open to receiving as much as giving. You will find people are more receptive to the love you give when you allow yourself to be a receiver. Taking small steps to be more open emotionally deepens the bond you will experience with someone. This may take getting beyond a fear to let someone know you on a deeper level, but the fulfillment awaiting you will be a great reward.

Denying Anger

The past-life pattern of denying anger will become a distant type of influence if you get better at letting your feelings be known. Emotional intensity is usually linked to the passion you want to express by letting your voice be heard. Cutting through layers of past-life memories in which your ideas were held back can be overcome by being more assertive. Your relationships find balance when you are more direct about being yourself. When you take steps to be in the moment with honest communication, there is less need to have anger building within you. The energy it takes to hide anger can be channeled into more productive directions. Sometimes it is the fear of letting anger out that needs to be overcome. You might be surprised that anger can bring people closer, as it brings a problem into the open so it can be solved.

Ruled by Guilt

The ruled by guilt pattern is playing off an instinct you have to fix the problems other people have created. If you learn to set limits on how much you can take on for others, this past-life pattern will not be a problem. Your energy levels and emotional strength are stronger when you are reasonable in helping people. You are a more reliable friend, family member, and lover when not allowing a feeling of guilt to rule you. Performing actions not based on guilt empowers your relationships.

Another way to resolve this pattern is by listening to your intuition when it is telling you not to embrace guilt. Eventually you will get good at perceiving individuals who seem to know how to manipulate you through guilt. Stopping this past-life pattern from occurring is liberating. Trusting your perceptions to let them guide you away from walking in the footsteps of guilt is your path out of this past-life pattern.

The Virgo Reward from Solving Karmic Patterns

You have the tenacity embedded in your mind to work your way through any past-life pattern. Think of it as starting a new project when it comes to walking on the path of overcoming any pattern you want to change. Each step you take will lead to more confident ones as you move away from the hold of a pattern. The result is you will notice your relationships will have greater flow. Communication between you and your closest allies will likely become clearer. Your sense of personal power will grow stronger as you come to grips with a pattern. Your tendency to act out a past-life pattern will lessen with patience and practice.

If any of the patterns discussed sounded familiar, don't worry. Remember that first you have to perceive a behavior before you can change it. You need not feel any pressure to change a past-life pattern overnight. If you use that Virgo determination to rise above a pattern's influence, you will come out the winner.

Don't make perfection your goal. Rather, see your efforts in dealing with past-life influences as a road to greater relationship fulfillment. The harmony and peace you hope to achieve are within your grasp as you begin the journey of self-discovery.

SEVEN
LIBRA: THE SOCIALIZER

Dates: September 22 to October 21

Element: Air

Strengths: Diplomacy, fairness, mediator

Challenges: Indecision, too compromising, too oppositional

Karmic Relationship Primary Shadow: Denying problems

Key to Transforming Karmic Patterns: Balancing intuition with
intellect

The Libra Current-Life
Relationship Landscape

If you were born under the sign of Libra, you have a natural way of
making others feel at ease. Your personality is outgoing, especially if
you are comfortable with social situations. The traditional astrology
phrase for Libra is "I balance." Keeping your own emotions and
mental energies in balance is important to your sense of comfort.

You appreciate people who are not overly demanding of your generosity. Individuals who know how to surprise you with pleasant experiences excite you. Those who infringe on your time can wear you out unless they are near and dear to your heart.

Romantic atmospheres are a way to your most intimate feelings. You long for a soul mate with similar interests. There will be certain goals or pastimes you need your lovers to support. If they appreciate your unique ideas, you will be a friend for life. You like to know people are listening when you speak. If you feel discounted, your anger is aroused quickly. You will hide your emotions from someone until you are sure they deserve to be informed of them.

Some people may perceive you as hard to please. You probably see this as having particular likes and dislikes that are not out of the ordinary. You will be patient to let a relationship develop. On the other hand you will pull back if a person gives you a good reason to no longer trust them.

You value partnership. There is an inner desire to want those important people in your life to be patient with you. You likely have a wide variety of acquaintances. Receiving inputs of new ideas from various sorts of individuals opens your eyes to greater options to realize your future goals.

The Libra Past-Life Karmic Relationship Patterns

Everyone has brought past-life patterns into the current life. It might make you feel better to know you are not alone. If you connect with one or more of the past-life patterns discussed, don't let it worry you. By acknowledging that a karmic theme has been part of your current incarnation, you are taking the first steps to transform the energy into a more productive expression. It does take patience to work your way through past-life influences that might be interfering with your relationship fulfillment. Think of the effort you make to discover better ways to make use of the past-life energy to have a happier and abundant life.

As a Libra, your passion to seek a balanced life can persuade any past-life energy to work in favorable directions. Your dedication to wanting a relationship filled with harmony will keep you on the right path. If you notice you are slipping back into the web of a past-life pattern don't get frustrated. Each time you start again to make peace with shadow forces from past lives, your insights will guide you to see the world with a renewed vision. When you release a past-life pattern, the road ahead is filled with the people you long to meet who share your dreams and need for love.

Sitting on the Fence

If this past-life pattern has become too activated in your current life, it produces a great amount of indecision when it comes to settling into a relationship. Libra is known for weighing decisions on a scale. There is nothing wrong with carefully contemplating if someone is right for you. The conflict does become a reality in this pattern if it causes you to fear making a commitment. It could be that in some past lives a repeating theme was never finding a sense of comfort as relationships grew closer. Usually the culprit gaining influence in this pattern is the inability to trust others. It may be not believing enough in yourself to sustain a relationship that requires emotional depth. This is not saying all your past lives showed you acting in this way, but only the ones linked to this pattern.

I Am Lost without You

When it becomes too dominant, this past-life pattern causes an extreme dependency on others. The real problem comes into being if you are too attached to someone who isn't paying attention to your own needs. The boundaries become very blurred to the point that you can feel like you are serving the life of someone else and neglecting your own. It is painful for a Libra to be in a partnership and feel too invisible when it comes to not getting the emotional support you desire. Your resources are getting poured into a person who doesn't appreciate the favor. Your goals can become distracted by the worry you feel in not getting the reassurance that someone is really there for you. If you stay in a state of denial about the reality of the relationship, it begins to drain you on the mental and emotional levels.

Too Compromising

As a Libra, you have a natural instinct to try to create fairness in your negotiations with others. If this past-life pattern emerges, you can find yourself going too far in trying to please people. This is especially true in your closest relationships. Emotions have a way of fogging your perceptions when you are afraid of disappointing someone. If you give much more than you receive to keep a person close to you, it might begin to throw a relationship out of balance. It could be a fear of causing anger if you disagree with a partner who keeps this pattern hovering over you. Tiptoeing around sensitive issues in your relationships is a type of behavior that compromises how you really feel. The result causes more problems than handling differences in a direct manner. The price you are paying grows bigger when you enable others to expect you to be overly accommodating.

Winning at All Costs

This is a pattern that becomes too operational in your life if you lose sight of opposing points of view. You perceive being challenged as a threat. It becomes too important to push your own ideas creating extreme tension in your communication with others. The love and intimacy you hope for become too absent. This carryover from some of your past-life experiences puts you on the defense probably more than needed. A fear of becoming too vulnerable is another way this past-life pattern enters the current life. You don't want to show any weakness, but you could be pushing away individuals that would make good lovers or friends.

Another way this pattern might manifest is through people you know. You are getting a chance to observe how this pattern you once displayed in past lives is working in someone else. The challenge is not walking backward into this pattern again or getting pulled into it by someone ensnared by this pattern in their own life.

Too Aloof

Libra is an air sign, which accentuates the mental side of life. This pattern can weave its way into your current incarnation if you too often allow your intellect to hide your emotions. The tricky thing about this pattern is that you could be completely unaware you are repeating a past-life scenario. The closest people in your life might perceive you as purposely not wanting to show your feelings. You may rationalize this as needing to stay mentally clear. The problem here is that you might seem uncaring when a person you care about needs emotional support. The intimacy and love you want to receive could be held back by a loved one if they can't connect with your inner world. Your comfort with communicating intellectual words and concepts has trouble transferring over to the feeling side of your mental circuitry. In your own mind you may think you are expressing yourself adequately, while someone close to you perceives you to be miles away.

Loss of Identity

As a Libra, you thrive on your people connections. This past-life pattern works its way into your current life if you depend too much on someone to confirm your identity. It could be that you are attracting friends and lovers with strong personalities that overly influence your goals. Your ideas get water thrown on them too much of the time. You might experience some confusion in defining what you really need from others to be happy. The assertion to speak with a confident voice is negated by those with louder ones. Giving in to who people think you should be rather than being yourself makes you feel like a stranger in a strange land. Accepting negative messages about yourself from manipulative individuals keeps the harmony you long for away from you. You came into this life to walk away from this pattern, but the portal out of this past memory remains a mystery.

Future Goal Confusion

If this past-life pattern becomes active in your life, you can be living too much through the goals of others. There may be a tendency to think you have to have the same future plans as those closest to you. A self-imposed peer pressure may be overly influencing your ideas about your future plans. The template others are using to define what they want from life has been superimposed on your own thoughts. A sense of stagnation can take place until you tune in to your own authentic needs. It isn't that you lack inner strength as much as alignment with your own passion. This pattern might find you overthinking rather than taking action. You could be too sensitive in letting the insights that work for others block your own.

Rigid Strategist

Libra is blessed with a strategy-oriented mind that can become a great asset for accomplishing a plan. This pattern occurs when you can't adapt to the goals of others to develop a shared path to success. It could be in some past lives you felt a need to hold on to your own ideas at all cost. Your memory of those lives is embedded in your consciousness but does not mean you have to act out this pattern of reasoning again. Your relationships will endure great tension if you are too attached to a strategy that can't allow you to hear what others need from you. Having mental toughness can be a true asset. But seeing the world through a fixed mindset makes it a challenge for people to get close to you. This pattern creates the likelihood that you will stimulate the differences between you and someone rather than finding a road that leads to harmony.

Fear of Commitment

If this past-life pattern makes its presence known, you could show a reluctance to let yourself get serious about a relationship. A challenge in trusting that you have found the right person for yourself could be a repeating event. You may like the idea of finding a soul mate but have trouble believing in the reality of finding a special person. Partnership is likely meaningful to you, as is friendship. When you start to become more emotional about a person, you suddenly hit the brakes. This is a past-life pattern lodged in your memory that, if activated, blocks you from falling in love. This pattern may be linked to a feeling of divine discontent that has you thinking there should be a perfect person waiting for you to discover. This can't occur because nobody is perfect.

Another possible appearance of this pattern is that it approaches you in the form of someone else displaying this behavior. This is your opportunity to perceive this influence in another individual but not to act out this shadow force yourself. In other words you came into this life to sidestep this karmic expression.

Ruled by Anxiety

Your sign Libra belongs to the mentally oriented air element. Your mental circuitry at times gets overloaded if you feel you are getting too much input from people. Your nervous system in close relationships intensifies if individuals appear to be leaning on you too heavily for their emotional needs. You may suddenly need to pull away to get your objectivity back. This past-life pattern surfaces more often when you don't take some space to reclaim your clear thinking. Your moods grow stronger when you aren't getting occasional alone time. Your emotional intensity could explode if you feel too pressured into making decisions. Having a strong intellect is in the natural energy of your sign. If you don't claim your own space in a relationship, your mental energy gets weaker. This past-life pattern gains in strength if you don't realize you can't always be expected to solve someone's problems.

Starved for Attention

Being born under a people-oriented sign like Libra can bring you to want to have your voice heard by a wide range of individuals. It is when the drive for attention grows compulsive that this past-life pattern gets activated. There might be a feeling you are being ignored by those people you are the closest to on a regular basis no matter how much admiration you receive. This is a signal this past-life pattern has come alive. There is nothing wrong with wanting to have your own ideas recognized and supported by those you care about. Usually this pattern has its roots in feelings of a deep insecurity. There may have been past lives in which you were too taken for granted. In those past incarnations your opinions may not have been valued. It is possible that in the current life the scale has tipped too far toward compulsively feeling a need for attention. You can keep asking individuals to prove over and over again they truly care about you no matter how much they are doing this. This is a pattern that can throw cold water on the warm intimacy you hope to have in relationships.

Masquerade

Each of us has a persona or mask we show to the public. It is our personal style and our way of socializing. This past-life pattern becomes a problem if you depend too much on presenting an image of yourself to others but never get beyond it. It keeps you from a true intimacy and a deeper emotional connection with someone. This pattern is not an issue in casual encounters. The interference from this past-life pattern causes trouble in the relationships you want to explore on a deeper level. There is a playful side of this pattern. It is only when you can't come out of the shadows of this past influence and into the light of revealing more of your inner world that you can miss out on a good relationship. You are likely having trouble trusting yourself and others enough to release the hold of this pattern of thinking.

Altered Perceptions: Libra Paths to Transforming Karmic Relationship Patterns

Feeling the weight lifted off your mind after letting go of a karmic pattern is wonderful. Your positive thinking about people could rise to a higher level. Your self-confidence to embark in a new relationship direction can get ignited. Your trust in your insights about others may become stronger. Whatever was a past-life memory block now opens up new stimulating energy. Giving and receiving love could feel more flowing. There is no turning back once you have moved yourself out of the line of fire from a pattern of behavior that was interfering with your happiness.

There is a likelihood that at least one of the past-life patterns discussed hits the mark with your own experiences. If this is true, don't judge yourself. Nothing is intended to pass a negative light on you. Memories from past lives that are not beneficial for this lifetime take practice and much patience to channel into a positive expression. Those first steps into a new direction might feel awkward. It is like learning new perceptions that elevate your insight to better grasp the awareness to navigate through a past-life energy. Think of it as bringing thought patterns out of the shadows into a new illuminating light. It is an opportunity to embrace a journey of self-discovery that can reward you with fulfilling relationship harmony.

Sitting on the Fence

This pattern sometimes is easier to handle if you take the risk of letting someone get to know you on a deeper level. If this past-life influence is a regular occurrence in your life, it will take you some determination to get more decisive. There is nothing to really fear. Often the indecision about a person is more frustrating than giving a relationship a chance to evolve. It does take time for a relationship to reveal itself. The love you want to share with someone requires being willing to face adversity. Every relationship takes some adjusting to one another's needs. The trust you need to have in yourself may be closer than you think. Love in many ways takes a leap of faith. There is probably a side of you that believes in reality testing a partnership. You could be using this pragmatism too early in getting to know someone. If you view a relationship as a process that will unfold naturally, it could get you to jump off the fence.

I Am Lost without You

This pattern will stop surfacing if you break the attachment to supporting someone else's life at the exclusion of your own. It will probably seem awkward as you put yourself first. You might even accuse yourself of being selfish, but it will take this to get your life back in balance. When you begin to put yourself in relationships that give you a feeling of equality, it is a rebirth. You are reclaiming your power and finding new vitality on the road to personal empowerment. You may have attracted controlling types of people in past lives and need to be vigilant in this life not to allow it to happen again. As you focus yourself in a new direction, this pattern will seem like something from the distant past. In finding a greater sense of yourself, there is less likelihood in getting lost in someone else.

Too Compromising

The too compromising pattern reveals you might need to put a stop to being too ready to give in to the demands of others. Your negotiating skills need to get stronger. If you can get past worrying about causing friction because you openly stand up for your opinions, you are at least halfway toward leaving this past-life pattern behind. People who truly want to develop a relationship based on a mutual sharing of power will not expect you to do all the compromising. When you get over a reluctance to be assertive, your relationships fall into a natural balance. The desire to seek fairness in your social interactions is a Libra trait. You will attract individuals with a similar quest for equality because you value having it in your relationships. If you perceive the need to be uncompromising when it comes to being treated as an equal partner in major decisions, this pattern will let go of you.

Winning at All Costs

The winning at all costs pattern can be turned away from a negative expression by tapping into that Libra strategic ability you possess to create win-win results. Rather than expending immense amounts of energy fighting constantly for your point of view, it is more productive to try to reach shared resolutions. Sometimes agreeing to disagree is another way to lessen the likelihood of this past-life influence coming into your life. Creating enough ground for you and others to be mutually supportive of goals is one of your strengths. Focusing your mental energy to pursue your dreams gets the support you want to receive when you do the same for others. It is great to passionately fight for your ideas. If you don't lose sight of the voice of those you care about, the harmony you cherish is never far away. Truly listening to someone as you state your case in a dispute puts this past-life pattern to rest.

Too Aloof

This pattern can be overcome by allowing others to discover your emotional world. You have a well-developed mental strength that only needs to let your feelings be expressed. Your lovers and friends want to come closer when your emotions are visible. It may be that you need to trust that appearing vulnerable to someone you love makes the intimacy stronger. Having the courage to reveal your inner world puts you in the driver's seat in overcoming this past-life influence. It might be that you think talking on a mental level is revealing enough. If you can accept the feedback from someone that they need you to communicate your feelings, this pattern weakens in its intensity. The path to greater fulfillment in your relationships is in the here and now when you begin talking with emotion as well as with your intellect.

Loss of Identity

The loss of identity pattern can get a course correction by not letting others talk you out of your goals. To confirm your identity, you need to trust your mental insights and intuitive instincts. Learning how to distinguish input you get from others that is useful from input that is negating your self-image puts you out in front of this pattern. You came into this life to stand up for your ideas. It is okay to let someone's advice help guide you. Just be sure in the end it is your own inner voice that has the last word. If you stop letting opinions from others manipulate your thinking, the result is your identity gets empowered. When you don't try to copy the life of someone else, you stay out of reach of this past-life pattern. It is okay to have individuals with strong personalities in your life. They can be uplifting and encourage you to accomplish great things. You only need to be sure to walk to the beat of your own inspirational insights to be true to your own identity.

Future Goal Confusion

The future goal confusion pattern only needs you to align with your own inspirational thinking. It is a good thing to take into consideration advice you are given by others. You will get empowered when making choices that reflect your own values and needs. When you live out your own goals, you are giving the universe more ways to offer you greater opportunities for abundance. The power of attracting opportunities with a promise of fulfillment helps you find a magical synchronicity when you launch out in independent directions. You will experience that your partnerships and friendships benefit from making choices that emanate from your own passion. There is a chance this past-life pattern has been hidden from your conscious mind. When you express your most authentic ideas for the future, this pattern will stay out of your current life.

Rigid Strategist

When you reach out to that balanced objectivity embedded in the fabric of Libra, the rigid strategist pattern becomes less likely to appear. Like a gifted chess player, you have an excellent ability to plan a few moves ahead in your thought processes. If you make your way of perceiving situations clear to others, it makes for a greater possibility of winning support. If you show you are listening and are willing to budge from your positions, people become more agreeable. It only takes a spirit of cooperation that allows your friends and lovers to climb on board with you. Giving your strategic advice when requested brings your special people closer. Sometimes it will be your allowing others access to your way of reasoning that takes the tension out of disputes. Remember that Libra is a mentally oriented air sign that needs to show they care about the feelings of others. It could be that your emotional expression lets others know you hear their voice right alongside your own, and that is the road to harmony.

Fear of Commitment

The fear of commitment pattern comes down to trusting that you deserve a fulfilling relationship. That usually is the first step to rising above the hold of this past-life influence. A close intimate relationship with someone may feel like less of a risk as you believe in what you have to offer a partner. Love can get messy as you go through the good and difficult times with a person. If you stay in a relationship long enough, this could reveal the happiness you hope to find. If this pattern is active in your life, it is very possible that it is linked to some past lives in which you felt betrayed in some way. It does not mean it has to happen again. If you stay positive and define clearly what you need from a relationship, this pattern's influence will lessen in a big way. If you don't worry about the commitment but pay attention to getting to know someone, it is a wiser path to follow. Think of being with a person as a journey of self-exploration as much as figuring out if you have found the right person. The mutual acceptance of each other may take some time, so enjoy each step of the path.

You may be attracting people who have commitment issues. It might be an opportunity to get a glimpse of a pattern you don't want to repeat in the current incarnation. It is the universe reminding you that it is a behavior you don't want to fall into.

Ruled by Anxiety

This past-life pattern is easier to manage if you don't take on too much responsibility in solving the problems of others. You stay mentally and emotionally stable when functioning as a reliable support system with clear boundaries. Your happiness in love and friendship rests upon having realistic expectations for yourself. You can't save someone from facing their own issues. Your relationships will stay in balance if you don't enable others to lean on you without putting in their own effort. You have valuable insights to share with those closest to you. When you have an equal footing in a relationship, this pattern has less of a chance to appear. There will be occasions when you need alone time to gather your thoughts. It is an innate need of being a Libra to know when to walk to your own drumbeat and when to take footsteps close together with someone you love.

Starved for Attention

The starved for attention past-life pattern might not be as easy to identify from your past-life memories. It can hide out of sight from your conscious awareness. It is important to realize you are a complete person without someone else. It is from here you can create the type of relationship that brings you fulfillment. Harmony with someone is closer than you might think. When you stay grounded in knowing you don't need another individual to complete you, your relating to others finds balance. Your sign thrives on partnerships that have a well-established equality. A barometer to know you have the right people in your life is that they don't want all of your attention. They will encourage your independence as much as wanting you to support their own unique goals. Paying attention to your own self-discovery attracts from the universe the relationships that bring you great harmony.

Masquerade

The masquerade past-life pattern only needs you to not be afraid to let others discover you on a deeper level. If you take the challenge of trusting someone, you could be surprised how good it feels. The intimacy and closeness rise fast in your relationships when you reveal more of yourself emotionally. Your ability to be a strong partner for someone makes you highly desirable in the eyes of many others. People really would like to know what lies behind the intellect you display. You don't need to rush yourself to open up if it is difficult. But taking a first step to express feelings as well as your intellect is a winning formula to put this past-life pattern to rest.

The Libra Reward from Solving Karmic Patterns

You will feel a great sense of accomplishment when facing a karmic past-life influence and rising above it. It is a great relief to do so, as it frees you to experience more harmony in your relationships. It is okay if you are only beginning to take the first steps on this journey. Sometimes it is becoming aware of any of these past-life patterns that opens your eyes to new ways to express this energy. The shadow forces embedded in a pattern do come out into the light of clarity when you recognize the potential of channeling the energy into productive directions.

It is in your Libra grasp to handle the challenges presented by a past-life pattern. You have a levelheadedness to navigate your way to a clear understanding of how to disengage from influences that are interfering with the harmony you seek in relationships.

There is a decisiveness within you to transcend a past-life pattern with a patient persistence. There is no competition to worry about in getting past a pattern. This is your own journey. Think of it as a self-discovery to create a wonderful highway to find your way to relationship fulfillment.

EIGHT
SCORPIO: THE TRANSFORMER

Dates: October 22 to November 21

Element: Water

Strengths: Sense of personal power, charisma, business skills

Challenges: Jealousy, power struggles, manipulative

Karmic Relationship Primary Shadow: Fear of the unknown

Key to Transforming Karmic Patterns: Integrating the past with new insights

The Scorpio Current-Life Relationship Landscape

If you were born under the sign of Scorpio, your way of perceiving the world is lined with emotional intensity. Your relationships are an important component on your road to self-discovery. You have a natural way of learning from real-life experiences. The traditional astrology phrase for your sign is "I empower." Your belief in some-one can motivate their self-confidence to help them pursue new goals. You do expect others to return their support for your own personal aspirations.

Relationships are a type of ritual in your belief system. You likely value loyalty, and it is the cornerstone for you to trust those closest to you. You detest betrayal because it feels like a stab in the back. You prefer emotional honesty most of the time. Although, it must be said at times you are not ready to handle the truth. You prefer lovers and friends to be patient with your decision-making. Some think you purposely take too long to make important decisions. You see this more as taking the time to carefully process the pros and cons involved. You like coming out the winner in negotiations but don't always like revealing this.

Passion comes from the depths of your emotions. You border on possessing a partner but at the same time want those you love to exert their independence. Sharing power with your lovers wins their admiration. There are those fearing your blunt spoken words about them. Many find your direct communication refreshing.

You can be generous with your mental and physical resources. You know how to empower with your facial expressions as much as your actions. Then again, you will hold back your support for those who don't appreciate you. You like being cherished but might push back against being too possessed by someone. You will open up your feelings if a person can be trusted. There are occasions when you need time to yourself, as privacy is sacred to your mind and soul. You do like being held in the arms of a lover. Finding a soul mate feels like a safe world and one worth treasuring.

The Scorpio Past-Life Karmic Relationship Patterns

You are not alone when it comes to bringing past-life patterns into the current incarnation. Our soul has traveled along a journey over several lifetimes. In some past lives a repeating pattern of behavior could have followed you into this life. These memories can become activated when we experience various relationship encounters. If you find yourself identifying with any of the past-life patterns discussed, don't see this as a judgment of yourself. In embarking on a path to gain clarity and new understanding about these shadowy energies, you are taking steps to new self-discovery.

As a Scorpio, you have the mental and emotional strength to overcome any of the past-life patterns. Your sense of personal power rises as you break loose from the hold of karmic patterns. It does require patience to stay determined to change a behavior into a more favorable light. Think of it as a learning experience to convert what was a pattern of behavior interfering with your relationship happiness into a positive expression. Enjoy the journey to greater knowledge.

Under My Thumb

When this past-life pattern becomes activated, there is a tendency to fear not being in control. What is the result of this thinking? Usually a Scorpio tendency is to want to overpower others. A territorial instinct wanting to be preserved will release bossy tendencies. It impedes your growth in relationships to establish a genuine intimacy. It is possible you don't realize this shadow lodged in your past-life memory is part of the way you handle yourself in relating to others. When challenged by someone, you could resist acknowledging you embrace this pattern. The love and happiness you hope for becomes a distant reality if you don't shake the hold of this past-life energy.

Another way this past-life pattern can come into your life is through someone else conducting themselves in this way. This is saying it might be a pattern you came into this life to overcome and you are seeing it in another person. You are getting a front row seat to realize you don't want to go down this path. Sometimes we attract someone who indulges in a past-life energy who we have come into the current life to conquer. It is critical to not come under the spell of that person.

Lost in Silence

Scorpio is a water sign, which denotes deep emotional energy. There can be instincts to hide your feelings. This pattern surfaces when you are having a difficult time with trust. Those people closest to you may wonder what you are thinking when trying to get you to talk. You could be perceived as purposely retreating into a state of hibernation when it comes to sharing your true opinions. It is a fact Scorpio individuals like yourself prefer to carefully process information. You may forget that others need you to come out of your reflecting so they can hear you verbalize your likes and dislikes. If you don't participate in enough communication, the intimacy you desire is not going to become a reality. Recharging your battery through taking some quiet time is normal. It is only when you use it as an excuse to hold back your feelings that this pattern intensifies and the love you need might lessen.

Angry Moods

This past-life pattern has its roots deep in hidden anger. Anger is a raw emotion, and if allowed to build with no release valve, eventually it will explode. If you don't let out intense feelings, they can interfere with your perceptions. Worse is your anger may be launched at someone over a situation unrelated to what you originally became upset over. Scorpio moods are a barometer about how you are feeling. They let you know how you are reacting to the behavior of others. It sometimes is better to let out your emotional intensity in the present. Another way this past-life energy can manifest is if you have a regular habit of trying to push others to always agree with you through acting out angry moods. You don't win the closeness you might hope to achieve. People will more than likely pull away when you display this pattern. An ocean of resentment from people is often the end result of falling into this shadowy energy.

Holding Grudges

Scorpio has an instinct to sometimes have trouble letting go of a person's past transgressions. They can be viewed as an absolute taboo. This past-life pattern finds new life if you continue to dislike someone even if they no longer are exhibiting the behavior that previously disturbed you. It can keep a relationship from growing if you let this pattern infiltrate your thinking. You don't have to forget how you don't like a person's past actions. But if you cannot forgive, there may be a rift between you and someone close that is hard to fix. It is even possible that this shadowy energy might drain your mental energy. Staying too often locked in this pattern is being attached to a negative thought pattern that keeps you from the happiness you want to have in a relationship.

Extreme Jealousy

If you allow this pattern into your current incarnation, it drives a wedge between you and a person you care about. It can be a case of not trusting someone even if they give you no reason to feel this way. The underlying reason for this pattern is often a fear of losing a lover or friend to someone else. It can be that you don't want to act like this but can't shake the influence of this shadowy force. It might be that camping out in your past-life memories are images of being abandoned or betrayed. This does not mean it has to occur in this life, but you are still being pulled back into those past memories. You lose your sense of personal empowerment if you keep giving in to this past-life pattern. Your own self-worth is getting lost in not feeling someone is truly valuing you. Your dependency needs become out of balance if you stay in this pattern of thinking.

There is another way this past-life pattern can approach you. Someone you know may be directing this jealous behavior at you. It may surprise you that a lover could not trust you. The key thing here to remember is that you are being given an opportunity to perceive this pattern in someone else but don't need to walk down this path yourself.

Denial

If it becomes too present in your life, this past-life pattern will find you denying what you perceive in a relationship, thinking it will keep the peace. If this becomes an ongoing event, you could be missing out on getting your needs met. There is a little denial in all relationships. But if you are going way beyond your limits to remain in a relationship, you are getting a bad deal. You are putting that Scorpio ability to do a reality check on the back burner, meaning you are only seeing what you want to see. Those insights you possess are getting too watered down, fogging your self-honesty. You could be enabling behaviors expressed by someone by not speaking truthfully about how their words and actions are impacting you.

This pattern can come to you through a person in denial about how they are treating you. It does not seem to matter how many times you speak up—the behavior continues. This could be a past-life pattern you acted out yourself in previous incarnations. You have attracted an individual who displays this pattern firsthand. The universe is trying to show you this is a past-life pattern you don't want to act out in your own life.

Overanalyzing

The Scorpio tendency to think through experiences deeply can go to an extreme, potentially opening the door to this past-life pattern. You could be looking too much for what could go wrong in a relationship. Your sign is known for processing your thoughts carefully. There is a chance you might not give a relationship enough time to develop before giving up on it. The fear of adversity could be what is activating this pattern. Rather than work through a problem with someone, the temptation to escape starts occupying your thinking. You may be creating a crisis without realizing you are doing it. If you have a habit of leaving a relationship due to not wanting to deal with your differences with a person, it may be linked to this pattern. By not trusting you can communicate more openly, you make establishing a clear commitment difficult.

Too Much Pessimism

This past-life pattern becoming too much a reality indicates lost hope in thinking you can find the right relationship. This could be due to disappointing experiences from past relationships in this life and very possibly those that occurred in past lives. As a Scorpio, you will feel the pain of a relationship that has ended very deeply. Your normal ability to process your way through a disappointing love or friendship gets stuck in this pattern. The residue from a past-life failed relationship might be compounding the problem of letting go of a current person. It probably is not so obvious that a past incarnation could be contributing to a delay in working your way through feelings you have for someone in the current life. Being too attached to a negative outlook might keep you from a relationship that promises harmony.

I Will Not Be Moved

It is natural for the sign Scorpio to defend its position on a decision. It is when you are not willing to consider any options that this past-life pattern can appear. Stubbornly standing your ground too much of the time eventually causes friction in a relationship. You may be dedicated to your own preferences to the point that compromise stays out of reach. The closeness you want with someone is difficult to have if you will not budge in your ideas as needed. That Scorpio instinct to want things on your own terms becomes a very dominant force if this pattern is too large an influence. It could be an underlying fear of not trusting others that keeps you holding hands with this shadowy force that prevents you from enjoying greater relationship fulfillment.

Twisting the Truth

If this pattern is too active in your life, there is a tendency to tell people what they want to hear. It is a way to manipulate others into doing what you need them to do. Honest communication is missing. You have a hidden agenda that is in your own best interest. This is a type of passive-aggressive pattern that in the end tends to backfire. It usually does not end up bringing the harmony you need with someone. This pattern is linked to hiding behind a persona you are displaying that only serves to cause confusion. Another theme running through this pattern is a fear of closeness. When this pattern is too active in your life, communication is intended to be a tool to keep others at a distance.

There is another way this past-life pattern could appear in your life. Someone you know well may be in the habit of showing this behavior. It could seem eerily familiar and make you feel uncomfortable when you are aware of the pattern. It is your opportunity to recognize it and not choose to make use of it in your own life.

Power Struggles

There are occasions when you need to defend your decisions. This past-life pattern manifests when you go to extremes on a regular basis to prove you are right. If you don't share power equally, it will be difficult to achieve harmony in your relationships. This pattern is often linked to a need to stay in control. Trusting someone enough to relinquish some of your power brings people closer. There is a strong maintaining instinct in Scorpio. If you perceive an individual as disrupting your comfort zones, a desire to stand your ground emerges. A failure to openly communicate and be open to opposing viewpoints brings great tension into your relationships. The energy it takes to resist compromising can drain your energy. Defining your territorial needs too rigidly keeps the love and intimacy at a distance.

Lack of Assertiveness

Self-doubt creeps into your life too much of the time when this past-life pattern gains strength. This is the repeat of a pattern from past lives of letting others negate your thoughts. Your goals are shut down and get taken over by the strong opinions of someone else. Your inner strength is there but held back by being too cautious. A fear of ridicule has you keeping your insights in the shadows. The faith to pursue your own dreams is missing. Being in the company of individuals with extreme self-interest will overshadow the footsteps you need to follow toward your own future goals. Living out the hopes and wishes of others stifles your own pursuits. Staying in limiting relationships keeps you from finding the love and acceptance in more fulfilling relationships.

Altered Perceptions: Scorpio Paths to Transforming Karmic Relationship Patterns

When you release a karmic pattern, the world seems to open up new possibilities for happiness and self-discovery. Your mental energy will feel invigorated. Positive thoughts are more likely to fill the vacuum left when you let go of a past-life pattern's influence. You may even find that intimacy and trust with others is easier to establish. The love you hope to experience can become a greater reality. Brave new perceptions can seem like a rebirth.

Don't be disturbed if one or more of the past-life patterns discussed sound like thoughts and actions you have acted out. Think of this as a learning experience. It is like a cosmic composting of taking negative energy and channeling it into more productive directions. Taking the first steps to confront a karmic pattern is the path to clearer insights. It can require practice and patience to get unentangled from a pattern from previous incarnations. Releasing the hold of this energy opens your mind to awakened ideas that can lead to relationship harmony. The confidence to overcome a past-life pattern will come faster than you might have imagined.

Under My Thumb

The under my thumb pattern can become less likely to occur if you stay away from controlling behaviors. It is natural for a Scorpio to have territorial needs. Letting those people you are closest to have their own sense of freedom empowers your relationships. When people know you trust them to make their own decisions, the communication flows more smoothly. Encouraging lovers and friends to exert their independence allows for intimacy to become a reality. This is a pattern that can hide from your conscious mind. Acknowledging this behavior brings it out from the shadows so you can begin to change.

There are occasions a past-life pattern becomes visible through someone you know. Having the awareness to not adopt this pattern for yourself keeps it from resurfacing in your own behavior. Sometimes we attract individuals acting out a pattern we have come into this life to overcome. If you are in a relationship with a person displaying this pattern, be happy you recognize this is not a behavior you want for yourself.

Lost in Silence

The lost in silence pattern only needs you to communicate more openly. When you don't expect people to read your mind and you talk openly, you allow people to come closer. Your emotions have a tendency to run deep. When you make a conscious effort to let someone into your inner world, the harmony you seek can happen. It may seem awkward at first if you are not good at expressing your ideas openly. With practice it gets easier. If you need some space, it is a good idea to tell someone. As a Scorpio, you highly value privacy. You could be surprised that a loved one might not mind you taking time to yourself. The key is when you are in the company of those you love and appreciate, be sure to stay visible. Be an active listener, as it does wonders for creating a bridge to a real shared, fulfilling relationship.

Angry Moods

The angry moods pattern is less likely to surface again in this lifetime through expressing your feelings more openly. It is true that in some instances you may need to cool down before overreacting to someone's words or actions. There is an emotional intensity linked to the passion you feel. Holding back anger for extended periods often enlarges an issue you have with someone. Having the trust that a person will not run away from you if you let out your true feelings comes with practice. Tuning in to your moods actually can put you in touch with your clearest intuitive insights. You likely are sensitive to the energy of other people. Getting some meditative time to yourself is a great way to calm down moods and stay centered. Anger in itself is not a bad thing and can indicate you have feelings that must be communicated. When you don't fear your emotional power, it puts you closer to rising above this pattern and opens the door to relationship fulfillment.

Holding Grudges

The holding grudges pattern only needs you to redirect what has been a negative use of a powerful memory ability into a positive direction. Rather than holding on to energy that is working against you, you will feel a fast sense of relief when walking out of this past-life pattern. It might take some conscious effort to move away from this pattern of thinking, but you will be glad you did. Your relationships will go more smoothly. The communication will have a flow that has a greater promise of mutual cooperation with someone. When you let go of negative perceptions of someone more quickly, the emotional closeness is easier to feel. The support for your goals will be there when you need it. The less you sit in judgment of others, the more likely they will be to do the same for you. The road to harmony with others has fewer obstacles when you break free from this pattern.

Extreme Jealousy

The extreme jealousy pattern frees you in many ways when you find the determination to let go of this tendency. When you establish your own unique sense of independence, this pattern disappears. Perceiving that jealousy only serves to take away from your personal power allows you a feeling of liberation. You will then attract the type of people you can trust. You will find clarity on the path to fulfilling relationships when you find the willpower to release jealous urges. The less you worry about what you could lose the more you are filled with new insights. You gain a new wealth of energy by rising above this past-life influence. Your dependency needs come into balance when you tap into your own self-worth. You enjoy your relationships more as you take the risk of trusting others and believing in your ability to pursue people who will be there when you need them.

If you happen to be in a relationship with a person caught in this pattern, you need to use that Scorpio insight to be aware of it. This may have been a past-life pattern you came here to overcome. Having the awareness to see this behavior in someone else is likely going to keep you from falling back into this past-life influence.

Denial

The denial pattern will be less of an issue if you admit to yourself that a behavior you perceive in someone must be faced. If you speak up and tell someone how their words and actions are impacting you, it is an empowering experience. You need to draw a line in the sand for what you can tolerate. Having inner peace and finding harmony in a relationship are within your grasp when you put denial behind you. If this has been a pattern shadowing you for a long time, you will need some persistent determination to walk away from its influence. You will get more of what you need from others when you move beyond staying in denial only to keep someone happy with you. If you are in the right relationship, your lovers and friends will be able to handle how you really feel.

It is possible this pattern is being presented to you through an individual you know. A person is in a state of denial about how they are interacting with you. Think of it as the universe giving you an opportunity to get a view of this pattern to allow you to realize you don't want to accept this as your own reality.

Overanalyzing

It is a good idea with the overanalyzing pattern to have as a mantra "there are no perfect people." It will keep you from worrying too much about the things you don't like to the exclusion of the positives. The ability to research and have in-depth insights is a valuable trait for Scorpio to display. Being harder on the problems than on a person is a wise path to follow as well. Taking the time to get to know someone could allow you to see the potential of a solid relationship. Relationships can get messy at times. By not letting the first sign of adversity make you retreat from a relationship, you gain inner strength. You have a wonderful capacity to communicate with a lover or friend on a deep level based on trust. The reward for warming up to a commitment outweighs the fear of adversity. The intimacy and happiness you can enjoy with a trusted partner may make this past-life pattern a faraway memory.

Too Much Pessimism

This pattern needs you to get a brighter outlook on finding partners that share what you value in life. This pattern challenges you to stop judging current people you meet based on what has happened in past relationships. What may not be so obvious are painful past-life relationship memories residing in your subconscious mind. This might be keeping you from believing in the possibility of finding someone you can find harmony with in this life. Taking those first steps in trusting that you deserve relationship happiness opens the door for new possibilities. The survival instincts are strong in Scorpio. Thinking positive awakens a rebirth in you. This can be the key to attracting the right type of person. You might be surprised how fast you can turn the corner away from this past-life influence with a new vibrant attitude.

I Will Not Be Moved

This past-life pattern needs you to show some flexibility. People respond to you with less resistance when you are willing to adapt to change. Trusting that it is okay to not have to willfully hold on to your normal way of doing things brings people closer. Letting others feel they are being included in major decisions is the road to harmony. It may take some practice to change this pattern of behavior, but you will find the effort will pay off. Truly listening and being open to new ideas adds an empowering quality to your relationships. This might be a past-life energy not so obvious to your conscious awareness. But you could be surprised that with some regular effort you will intuitively awaken to awareness by rising above this past-life pattern.

Twisting the Truth

The twisting the truth pattern can be less of a force in your life when you become a straight shooter in communicating with people. It can feel like a really scary leap of faith to trust someone. The interesting thing is that it takes less energy to be honest with others than to continuously have a hidden agenda. Those first steps toward opening up in a truthful way may feel awkward at first. It is like developing a new habit by retraining your mind to not hide what you need from someone. Surrendering a tendency to manipulate when communicating allows for true intimacy and a closeness you can trust.

If this pattern is being presented to you through the actions of someone else, consider it an opportunity to realize you don't need to act it out yourself. This could be a past-life energy that you came into this life to overcome. By seeing it in someone else, you can make a decision not to walk back into this past-life influence.

Power Struggles

The power struggles past-life pattern is less likely to reoccur if you realize you don't need to always be right. This pattern becomes less of a reality if you share the wealth of your power. It may sound strange, but as you empower others, you strengthen your own personal power. It takes much less energy out of you when you don't constantly force your ideas on others. Your passion for your own way of perceiving the world can inspire people to pursue their own goals. Being more of a team player is a path to creating harmony in your relationships. When you don't fear appearing vulnerable, people want to share their own inner world with you. Showing that you trust your intimate partners and friends wins their admiration. Allowing those you care about to chase after their own dreams ensures that this past-life pattern will stay dormant.

Lack of Assertiveness

The lack of assertiveness pattern has less of an impact in your life when you don't allow others to negate your insights. Taking the risk to promote your own goals pushes this past-life pattern out of the way. It is true that, as a water sign, the emotions of Scorpio can sensitize you to the energy of others. It might take some practice, but eventually as you speak with conviction, people will listen. Trusting your own intuitive inner voice will help you rise above individuals too critical of your opinions. The equality and harmony you want to find in relationships become a reality when you walk with self-confidence. When you step out of the shadows of someone else's self-serving dreams, you will discover like-minded souls who support your own dreams.

The Scorpio Reward from Solving Karmic Patterns

It can be a surprise to realize a past-life pattern has been active for quite some time in your life. Don't judge yourself. The effort you make in overcoming a past-life influence pays great dividends. Your relationships will come into a clearer balance as you gain insight about any past-life shadowy energy. As your understanding comes out into the light, a past-life pattern will be less bothersome. Scorpio has a great capacity to take energy that has been working negatively to a higher productive level. This can be experienced as a type of rebirth giving a new vibrancy in how you relate to others.

You likely saw yourself in one or more of the past-life patterns discussed. Remember they have no real control over you. With practice and patience, the self-discovery is exciting. You might even wonder why it took so long to convert a past-life energy into creative and fulfilling outlets.

There may be occasions when you question whether you are making enough progress in dealing with a past-life pattern. Think of it as a magical journey allowing you energized mental and emotional vitality. Your eyes will open to a world with more options to participate in relationships with a promise of love and harmony.

NINE
SAGITTARIUS: THE OPTIMIST

Dates: November 22 to December 20

Element: Fire

Strengths: Adaptability, open to new ideas, inspiring positive thinking

Challenges: Procrastination, fear of commitment, too judgmental

Karmic Relationship Primary Shadow: Loss of idealism

Key to Transforming Karmic Patterns: Staying open minded

The Sagittarius Current-Life Relationship Landscape

If you were born under the sign of Sagittarius, your insatiable optimism makes you very likeable. There is an urgency in you at times to share your thoughts with others. Gaining knowledge must be included in your regular mental diet. People who are bold in expressing their viewpoints get your attention. Closed-minded individuals might annoy you. Your lovers and friends like your expansive search for adventure and various kinds of new experiences. A traditional astrology slogan for Sagittarius is "I explore."

You are proud of your individualism and appreciate those who recognize this in you. Your idealism is passionate and inspiring. You thrive on having a like-minded partner and yet want to encourage independence. You like being depended on for advice but grow weary of people who lean too heavily on you.

Boredom is likely what you detest the most. You enjoy someone who challenges your ideas without judging you. Traveling with a lover on the mental and physical planes keeps life interesting. You might suddenly surprise someone with a new plan. If you give some advance notice of your desire for change, it stabilizes your relationships.

Patience is sometimes challenging, as you do have a restless spirit. You need multiple outlets for a creative mind. People probably perceive you as always being on the move, but you see this as a normal way to function in the world. When you take time to pause, you allow others to keep up with you and catch their breath.

Your loyalty wins the hearts of those you love. There is a sincere caring look in your eyes that individuals closest to you cherish. When you move forward to pursue goals and don't lose sight of your loved ones, harmony surrounds your relationships.

The Sagittarius Past-Life Karmic Relationship Patterns

Everyone has some past-life memories they brought into this incarnation. You probably will identify with one or more of the past-life patterns that will be discussed. Don't let this worry you. Each of us has come into this life with lessons to learn. Think of it as an adventurous journey to self-discovery. It helps to keep patience in mind as you read about the past-life patterns associated with your sign. If one of these past-life influences has been active in several past lives, it takes practice to express the energy in a positive direction. Becoming aware of a past-life pattern allows you to take steps toward gaining a new understanding.

As a Sagittarius, your desire to seek stimulating insights can guide you to overcome any past-life influences. You have a never-ending optimism that is your key to responding to challenges. There is an inner quest in you to find a soul mate and supportive friends. It is these people connections that give you the confidence to rise above a karmic pattern. The drive to find new routes to greater knowledge gives you the vision to navigate through any past-life influences.

Too Judgmental

Sagittarius is known for being open to input from other people. If this past-life pattern becomes awakened, your tendency to be closed minded can intensify. When you fight for an idea in a dogmatic way, you alienate the individuals you are trying to win to your side. It is refusing to listen to opposing points of view that creates tension in your relationships. If you become too much of a critic, you cause others to distance themselves from you. It is okay to fight for your ideals. Where the problem comes into being is when you lose your objectivity. That tolerance to let people express themselves freely is missing. A rigid and inflexible attitude interferes with the harmony you want in your relating to others.

Grass Is Greener Elsewhere

This past-life pattern has its roots in running away from a current relationship and thinking there is a more perfect one waiting somewhere else. This can cause you to leave a promising relationship too early before it has had a chance to develop. Sagittarius is a fire sign, and occasionally that impatience for situations to develop quickly is not realistic. The future seems more exciting than solving the everyday problems that can exist in even the best of relationships. Running away from what you believe to be too messy to search for, such as that just-right partner, is what is at the heart of this pattern. This past-life influence is like a revolving door that will keep you suddenly jumping out of relationships. It will keep you on the run until you face that this past-life pattern is taking you away from the fulfillment you hope to achieve with someone.

Hidden Emotions

At first glance you may appear easygoing and not difficult to get to know. If this past-life influence grows too dominant, your emotions may be a challenge to express. It might feel like someone has to pry open where your inner world resides. A fear of revealing your emotions is what is holding you back. You may find it easy to talk about a wide variety of subjects. Staying on the mental level is your natural comfort zone. The trust a partner wants to have for you could be difficult to achieve if they sense you are holding back your feeling side. Not wanting to appear vulnerable likely is at the root of this pattern. It may be hurtful feelings leftover from relationships in previous incarnations that keep you stuck in this pattern of behavior. This is a shadowy energy that can keep the love from flowing between you and someone you care about.

Commitment Confusion

Sagittarius has an inner wanderlust and travel urge. You might say these two traits keep you energized and enthusiastic about life. This pattern comes alive if you take the freedom principle too far. In other words, if this past-life influence grabs you with too strong a grip, you may be an unpredictable free spirit. Someone who wants more of a clear commitment from you might seem unreasonable. Your idea of a commitment may be to come and go as you please. If you want to keep someone close, they might have trouble accepting your definition of a commitment. Being depended on for emotional support makes you nervous when this pattern is a dominant force.

Another way this past-life pattern might appear is that someone you are involved with is displaying it. You may have a hard time knowing if you can count on this person when you need them. Consider this an opportunity to get a close-up view of this as a pattern you don't want to express yourself. It could be a past-life pattern you came into this life to escape.

Not Agreeing to Disagree

When activated, this pattern finds you fighting for your own ideas to the exclusion of truly listening to those of others. When you lose perspective by not considering alternatives to your own way of thinking, you create distance with people. Your communication tries to drown out the words of those trying to engage you by sharing ideas. This past-life pattern influences you to take one-sided views of situations. It can keep arguments on fire with no resolutions in sight. Compromise is difficult to reach. Instead of love and intimacy with a partner, you can end up with a broken heart. Sagittarius gives you a mental insight that can think a few moves ahead like on a chessboard. You have to ask yourself what it is worth to always play to win only what is best for you. This isn't the way to bring harmony into relationships.

Too Unpredictable

Your sign is one with a spontaneous mind that at times loves the thrill of new adventures. If this past-life pattern manifests in full force it can disrupt the close connection you have with someone. You might quickly surprise a person on a regular basis with wanting to make a major change of direction. If you are never giving much advance notice about changing your mind, a lover may feel left out of your future plans. You may appear to be too difficult to be counted on when someone needs you. This may be a pattern residing in your memory bank from lives when you were a free spirit, moving with no desire for roots. It could be you are still playing off these memories. Your lovers and friends may perceive you as too self-centered, while you think of this as living out your dreams. It can be a big challenge to have any stability in being with someone if you forget to let them in on your life script. It is that sudden urge to live on impulse that may make keeping those close to you along for the ride difficult.

Denying Issues

Hearing only what you want to hear can bring this past-life pattern into your everyday life. Issues that could be resolved quickly with honest communication get bigger when the discussion gets postponed to a later date. The optimism of Sagittarius can be used to act like there is nothing wrong in a relationship, but in reality a problem is driving a wedge between you and someone. A happy face you are wearing is trying to cover up dealing with adversity. Rather than work toward a solution, there is a tendency in this pattern to hold back how you are really feeling. The mystery of trying to figure out how you are sizing up a situation can cause unclear communication. The fear of causing an argument is often worse than directly dealing with a situation as it presents itself. The natural spontaneity of Sagittarius is getting blocked up by being too much in denial about negotiating clearly.

Fixation on Limitation

It seems like quite a contradiction for an optimistic Sagittarius to have a life dominated by lost hope. If this past-life pattern has too big a say, it is difficult to see the cup at least half full. You may think because you have run into some bad luck regarding relationships, you can't get things to turn around in your favor. It is very possible that embedded in your mind are memories that can be traced back to past incarnations when you ran into some relationship disappointments. The problem is that if this past-life pattern gets activated, you could be stuck too much in negative memories about relationships from lives in past incarnations rather than having a positive outlook about the current life. Instead of focusing more on what is good in your life, your mind is crowded by what is going wrong. The negative attitude is blocking the entrance of new people into your life.

Very High Expectations

Your belief in someone can bring out their best. But if you regularly have unrealistic expectations of them, it can be a sign this past-life pattern has emerged. There is a natural optimism in Sagittarius that can work great for your own life. If superimposed on someone else, it might be too far out in front of their reality. Others start to feel you are being too pushy about what you think is right for them. This can result in resentment and a tension that alienates those you are trying to help. Your enthusiasm that is meant to encourage can push someone away. Your idealistic belief in a person can become too much of a mission that invades the space of someone you care about.

It is possible that someone close to you is embodying this pattern. They may have good intentions but are not aware of their overencouraging you in a direction you don't want to go. Even when you try to talk to them about their behavior, it continues. Think of it as an opportunity to not accept this pattern for your own life. This could be a past-life pattern you came into this life to overcome, and the universe is letting you perceive it in someone else.

My Way Is the Only Way

Sagittarius is known for having an openness to a wide variety of ideas. Where this past-life pattern comes into play is if you expect your own ideas to always rule the day. This does cause a lover to keep you at arm's length much of the time. Usually the source of this pattern is a need to stay in control of the dialogue. A lack of trust can be another contributing factor giving this past-life shadow too much presence in your life. The tolerant quality found in Sagittarius that allows you to consider the ideas of others with a mutual acceptance is missing. This way of operating in the world makes the odds of finding harmony in relationships less likely.

Self-Serving Goals

If this pattern becomes activated in this life, a great "me" focus can grow very strong. You will lose sight of what others need from you. Your own goals come first too much of the time. You may expect support for your own future plans but are not paying attention to those of someone close to you. A compulsive drive for attention will begin to make people pull away. Sometimes it can be a cause a Sagittarius is dedicated to that might get you to expect a loved one to always put their own plans on hold. When you lose your perspective by only focusing on your own needs, you throw your relationships out of balance. The mutual respect for each other's ideas is missing.

Making Too Many Promises

Your sign sometimes bites off more than it can chew when it comes to making promises. It may not be so obvious in your mind that you have this tendency. The driving force behind this pattern is wanting to please others. The problem comes in when you have made promises and exaggerated your potential to fulfill them. The disappointment resulting from making unrealistic pledges serves to get people upset with you. This pattern could be traced back to past lives in which you had a fear of losing a lover. Trying to do too much made any issues between you and someone else bigger. This may be a type of pattern caused by avoiding honest communication about a problem with someone. To make the issue go away, the idea is to promise more than you can deliver, hoping it will make things better. It only delays really working out a disagreement.

Altered Perceptions: Sagittarius Paths to Transforming Karmic Relationship Patterns

There is a renewed revitalization of mental and physical energy when letting go of the hold of a past-life pattern. It can feel like your way of relating to others has gained new insights. You could even find yourself redefining what you need in a relationship. Your sense of empowerment often is enhanced through gaining clarity about past-life patterns. There is a possibility your insights about people will climb to a higher altitude. There is a journey of self-discovery stimulated when responding to the challenge of balancing past-life energies.

Don't get disturbed if one or more of the past-life patterns discussed seems like part of your current-life reality. Each of us has brought in past-life memories. The key thing to remember is that it takes patience to work through a past-life pattern. The first step is to awaken to the realization that a pattern from your past-life history may still be with you. You can then begin to find ways to not let it interfere with the harmony you hope to achieve. You have the capability to overcome any of the past-life patterns.

Too Judgmental

The too judgmental pattern only needs your sharp ability to exercise patience when seeing the flaws in someone's thinking. Letting someone speak without interrupting their flow of reasoning is more effective in getting them to hear your own logic. That Sagittarius ability to allow for more than one right answer to a subject of interest wins you greater cooperation. You are known as the student and teacher of the zodiac of signs. You stand a better chance to gain the knowledge from others when keeping an open mind. Rather than criticizing someone's opinions too strongly, let your mind stay objective. Giving others the freedom to speak even if you don't agree with them is a faster road to harmony. Acknowledging a lover's or friend's insights is a sure way to get them to accept your point of view.

Grass Is Greener Elsewhere

This pattern is asking you to slow down and let a relationship have enough time to develop. There is an inner restlessness in all fire signs like Sagittarius. The spirit of adventure in your sign only needs to be channeled clearly. It is possible that in some past lives linked to this incarnation you were not comfortable in a long-term relationship or there were circumstances that prevented this from occurring. In the current life this memory might still be with you. There is a better chance you will find a deeper sense of fulfillment if you give a relationship long enough to reveal its true depth. This past-life influence will lessen in intensity as you trust yourself enough to form a commitment in a relationship. Freedom is important to a Sagittarius. If you are in the right relationship, chances are your partner will value their own independence. When you get over fearing a stable relationship, you are most of the way there in rising above this pattern from past lives.

Hidden Emotions

The hidden emotions pattern is easier to resolve when you get over a fear of letting someone know you on an emotional level. You may not even know on a conscious level that your intellect is glossing over your emotional nature. Opening up to this awareness is the first step to overcoming this past-life influence. Conversing about many different topics is always at your fingertips. You like to know what people are thinking. Sagittarius can become quite emotional when expressing idealism and love for a cause. When you show your most intimate partners your feelings, they trust you in a big way. Fire signs like yourself sometimes project strength to avoid appearing vulnerable. You may be surprised that many will find you even stronger when you let them into your feeling world.

Commitment Confusion

The commitment confusion past-life pattern plays off your drive for wanting plenty of space to be yourself. If you are clear in respecting a partner's need to have the room to explore their own goals, you are well on your way to keeping this pattern from emerging. Making sure you are truly listening to what those closest to you need from you helps keep balance in your relationships. Often people just want to know you are hearing their voice. If you act like a team player, your lovers and friends stay happier. It might be that you pull away when someone wants a more defined commitment. Getting past a fear of closeness is the key to loosening the hold of this pattern.

There is a possibility you have met this past-life pattern through someone else expressing it. This actually may be a past pattern from some of your other lives that you came here to transcend. Think of it as an opportunity to get a viewing of this pattern and a chance to not accept it as part of your own reality.

Not Agreeing to Disagree

This pattern becomes less likely to make an appearance in your life when you consider what is best for you and someone else. There is nothing wrong with fighting for your beliefs. Just be sure to think in terms of fairly considering the opinions of others. You will find you can persuade others to your way of thinking when letting them talk freely. There is a spontaneous emotional intensity in Sagittarius that can have an appeal. Your ideas are more readily accepted when you show you are willing to listen to alternative points of view. Your sign attracts support for your way of thinking when you keep the talk flowing in both directions. Staying aware of the impact of your words allows you to maintain a broad, tolerant objectivity.

Too Unpredictable

The too unpredictable pattern does not have to come between you and those you love or want to maintain a relationship with in this life. Being born as a Sagittarius does give you an inner restlessness that at times will find you wanting to make changes quickly. If you can give some advance warning, there is a better chance someone will be more open to the new plan. If you keep your mind occupied with enough mental stimulation, it could settle down impulses that disrupt your relationships. There is a need for a Sagittarius to have their eyes on being there for someone in the present as much as on future goals. Balancing a propensity to move fast with being patient with others is a key theme to keeping this past-life influence away from you.

Denying Issues

The denying issues pattern requires a change in how you approach problems that arise in a relationship. Taking those first steps to not hold back when you need to speak up about a disagreement may take some practice. There will come a time when your response time will get faster. This past-life influence has less of a chance to manifest when you are more direct in communicating your thoughts. Much is gained when you offer your input and exchange ideas in a mutually beneficial way. Your thoughts on a subject often have a broad perspective that proves valuable. Finding that inner Sagittarius confidence to let your thoughts be visible may be met with a positive reaction that surprises you. This past-life pattern is linked to how much you feel comfortable with sharing your insights. There are going to be tense situations in any relationship. There are times when anger releases emotions that clear the air between people. The main thing to remember is that honest communication is more likely to get you closer to harmony.

Fixation on Limitation

The fixation on limitation pattern needs a refocusing of negative thinking into a new positive framework. The universe has a way of opening up new opportunities when you make room for them with a refreshed outlook. You don't need to settle for past memories, whether from this life or previous incarnations. There is a river of optimism always flowing within a Sagittarius like yourself. It only takes concentrating more on what could go right than on what could go wrong to bring new people into your life. There is luck in your sign that gets stronger when you believe in yourself. There is a magical synchronicity, which means meaningful coincidences, when you believe in abundance. You can cross over faster than you might think into a richer life surrounded by supportive people. It only takes those first few steps to keep a gratitude list in your mind. The universe will meet you halfway when you walk along a path of a positive energy.

Very High Expectations

The very high expectations pattern needs you to keep in mind that people you are close to have to go at their own pace. Your dreams may not be their own. You don't need to fix their imperfections any more than you would want them to try to do this for you. It is great to encourage and inspire others. Be reasonable about what you expect and this past-life pattern does not become an issue. Your idealism at times becomes strong, and you will want to lift others up. Just be sure you reality check to confirm you don't go too far beyond your own boundaries if someone is not asking you to do so. Letting someone know you are there for them as needed is a wise path to ensure balance in your relationships.

If it is true an individual is too demanding of you based on their own expectations, you will need to push back and let them know. It could be you are getting a glimpse of this pattern that you came into this life to overcome. It is your chance to gain the understanding that this is a past-life influence you don't want to put into your self-expression.

My Way Is the Only Way

This pattern is a closed way of perceiving the ideas of others that needs a more expansive view. Your relating to people gets a wonderful boost of energy when you stay away from dogmatic viewpoints. You attract the people who want to create harmony with you when you stay flexible. Surrendering controlling behaviors keeps those you love close. It is easier to rise above the issues that you and those you love face when you listen with an open mind. Your sign has a built-in capacity to accept people the way they are rather than pushing for your own agenda. The fulfilling relationships you can enjoy come to you when you make a concentrated effort to listen to alternative insights. It is the sure way to keep this past-life influence a distant stranger.

Self-Serving Goals

To overcome the self-serving goals pattern, don't let your passion for what is important to you overshadow what the main people in your life value for their own future. It is wonderful to pursue your own passionate interests. Encouraging your lovers and friends to go after their own dreams wins their admiration. Having some shared projects goes far in empowering your relationships. That Sagittarius enthusiasm when offered to others is highly appreciated. Your belief in someone gets them to want to support your own goals. Sharing your knowledge with individuals has a way of bringing great companions along your life journey.

Making Too Many Promises

This pattern needs you to be reasonable about what you can do for others to make them happy. It keeps your relationships in balance when the give and take is equal. There is the possibility for overconfidence in believing you can do the impossible for someone. Doing a reality check before trying to please someone is wise. Rather than not dealing with an issue with a person, you might be surprised to find it easier to talk over a problem. The direct approach takes less energy than making unrealistic promises. Chances are the intimacy and harmony are easier to achieve when you have the confidence to work through a problem. Keeping that Sagittarius desire to make someone happy to a reasonable level is the path to keeping this past-life tendency in check.

The Sagittarius Reward from Solving Karmic Patterns

The world would be missing a bright-eyed optimistic influence without the sign Sagittarius. Your ability to see the cup at least half full gives you the edge in overcoming any past-life pattern. It does take your fiery, feisty energy to not lose confidence in taking those first steps to navigate through a pattern's influence. Patience is important because some past-life memories have a tendency to hang on to us longer. You can outlast these past-life energies and win them over into a positive expression.

If one or more of the past-life patterns discussed sounded like they are part of your self-expression, don't let it worry you. Each of us has past-life shadow forces we are trying to gain clarity about. Be glad you are awakening to a new possible way of expressing these energies and thought patterns.

A fire sign like Sagittarius can get in a hurry to solve a problem. Try to remember that overcoming a past-life pattern takes time. The more awareness you gain about a pattern, the less influence it has. The persistent effort to seek self-growth will guide you to the relationship harmony and joy you hope to discover.

TEN
CAPRICORN: THE PRAGMATIST

Dates: December 21 to January 19

Element: Earth

Strengths: Clear ambition, reliable, focusing power

Challenges: Rigidity, too emotionally hidden, irrational fears

Karmic Relationship Primary Shadow: Old perceptions blocking a new reality

Key to Transforming Karmic Patterns: A commitment to new self-discovery

The Capricorn Current-Life Relationship Landscape

If you were born under the sign Capricorn, you are attracted to individuals with a sound logic. Those who show they understand your serious goals are appreciated. The traditional phrase in astrology for Capricorn is "I build." You are a steady planner and believe in finishing what you begin. You take commitments seriously and like people who honor them. You are more hardworking than many people you encounter. Ambition likely came early in life. You attract responsibility because you appear trustworthy and responsible.

When you trust someone, you expect this in return. There can be a cautiousness in beginning love or friendship types of relationships. Some people may perceive you as being emotionally reserved. You likely see this as wanting to make sure someone is worth revealing yourself to. You can be depended upon during a crisis, which is admirable. There is an inner strength that manifests during adversity that may even surprise yourself.

People with business sense are appreciated. You like grounded people with clearly defined goals. Then again, being surprised by those you love can warm your heart. You have an ability to focus on a goal that is the envy of the other astrological signs. There is a possibility that a special person in your life would be encouraging you to be more flexible.

Sharing your wisdom with others brings them closer. If you don't try to be too controlling, the intimacy and harmony you hope for are within your grasp. When you show unconditional love, romance and friendship come to greet you.

Your persona might display a serious face. When you let down your guard, you invite people to get to know you on a deeper level. You have a tendency to test the reality of your goals. In many ways you believe in trust but verify. Your relationships flow better when you are at ease with your life journey. Having a soul mate to celebrate anniversaries and special milestones with makes taking a chance on someone worth every bit of the effort.

The Capricorn Past-Life
Karmic Relationship Patterns

Don't have any anxiety about whether you will identify with any of the past-life patterns that are discussed. Everyone has brought in past-life material to work on. Keep a positive attitude. Any past-life energy takes some practice to gain greater awareness in understanding it. You gain empowerment in channeling a past-life pattern into a productive expression. Taking those first steps of bringing past-life influences out of the darkness into the light of clearer insight is the path to self-discovery.

As a Capricorn, you have that steady disciplined approach to life pursuits. You can take that sure footedness to solve a past-life pattern and open the door to more fulfilling relationships. It is not uncommon to wonder if you are making progress in rising above a past-life shadowy energy. If you keep your mind away from overanalyzing, you will find the journey that much more pleasant as you tune in to the clear vision to make peace with a past-life pattern.

I Am the Boss

This pattern is one in which you are leaving out the opinions from others due to exclusive loyalty to your own. This is a tendency that might be hidden deep in your memory and not so obvious to your conscious awareness. The impact of this pattern is to keep the closeness in relationships difficult to establish. A failure to listen to people's viewpoints can isolate you from receiving information that might be helpful to consider. The underlying source of this pattern is often an inability to trust. Others find it a turnoff when they realize you don't hear their voice about important decisions affecting you both. That shared feeling of mutual respect is missing.

Rigid Focus

If this pattern gains too much influence, it is a product of your great focusing power on ideas but your lack of flexibility. This type of thinking has a tendency to alienate individuals you are trying to bring closer. Intimacy and love get blurred if you hold on to this past-life shadow. Commitments are harder to keep strong with lovers and friends if they regularly perceive you as unwilling to ever compromise. Your dedication to a plan may be a good thing but causes problems if you forget to support the needs of those who care about you. If you stay too protective of your own insights and block out those of others, it causes great tension in relating to others

On My Guard

Capricorns can be very hesitant about revealing emotions to others. It can feel like you are losing your sense of personal power if you show feelings. If this way of thinking grows extreme, it is a sign that this past-life pattern has become activated. When you are too guarded, there appears to be a wall between you and someone else when they try to read your inner world. Your communication is more comfortable on the business level but stalls on the emotional highway. You could be expecting others to guess what is on your mind rather than communicating openly. The rings in the sky that surround your ruling planet Saturn in a similar way are guarding those feelings that come from the heart.

Conditional Love

There is a strategy side of Capricorn that serves you well in nego-tiating and that can be of great benefit to you and others. This past-life pattern could make an appearance if you are not going to express love for someone without any conditions. You may be over-structuring your giving affection to someone without getting what you need from them first. This does not create the closeness and harmony you hope to have. There is a lack of letting the love flow spontaneously between you and those you care about. People need you to be less agenda motivated and more spontaneous in sharing love. The more you make rules to guide your outpouring of love toward someone, the less likely you are going to find the fulfillment you seek in relationships.

Addicted to Negative Thinking

When your mind is working in the right direction and playing off positive energy, there is nothing you can't accomplish. If this past-life pattern gets kick-started, your negative thinking becomes too much in charge of the way you see the world. This can interfere with how you perceive the actions of others, causing you to do so in a way that is too judgmental. Your words then have a tendency to arouse anger rather than harmony when trying to make decisions with people. It is very possible you are looking for too much perfection in others. Love and fulfillment are not easy to have with a lover or friend if you accent the negative and set impossible standards.

This is one of those past-life energies that could come into your life through someone close to you. There is a chance you came into this incarnation to make peace with this pattern of behavior. The key thing to remember is not to get hooked into this past-life shadow yourself. The universe is giving you an opportunity to recognize this pattern in someone else and not make it part of your own reality.

Weak Assertiveness

An indication this past-life pattern has become activated is if your assertiveness in relating to others freezes up too much of the time. It is true a trait of Capricorn is wanting to carefully make sure an idea will be a success before making it visible to others. In relationships you could become frustrated if it seems like your goals are not valued. You may be overly attached to a past-life memory of when not getting your needs met was a regular event. This may be how this energy finds an opening into the current incarnation. Others can take advantage of the patience and reserved tendencies in an earth sign like Capricorn when your assertiveness is registering too low. Eventually this might turn into hidden anger if you allow someone to keep pushing your goals backward rather than forward.

Too Austere

Your expectations of people become too strict if this past-life pattern becomes too prevalent a force in your life. Too much of a rule orientation can stunt the growth of a relationship. This pattern keeps you from being able to walk in someone else's shoes to tune in to their perspectives. Usually this type of behavior puts great distance between you and someone else on the emotional level. Your own insights have a tendency to tightly block out those of other individuals. There is too much of a strict adherence to your own belief system when this pattern is activated. The natural evolving growth of a relationship is stifled. Communication breakdowns usually result when living in the walls of this past-life pattern.

Workaholic

This past-life pattern can manifest in more than one way. Capricorn can get so focused on work that people can feel neglected. An unwillingness to pay attention to those depending on you due to being totally distracted by work goals could be a problem. Losing that balance between dedication to a job or career and maintaining your personal life might keep you from giving time to a lover. Your commitment to work in this pattern excludes a commitment to a relationship.

There is another path this pattern can take: trying to work on others to change them into how you want them to fit your own image of them. This is a type of controlling behavior that weakens the bond you can form with a person. Blocking someone's own autonomy to be their own person usually results in a person revolting against you.

Sad Outlook

If you become entrapped in this past-life memory, it may influence you to look for the flaws in others and overlook their positive traits. Negativity is too much ruling your perspective about relationships. Rather than encouraging growth in someone, you are being too critical. The love you hope for is difficult to attain when you embrace this pattern. This can be a way of sabotaging a relationship to keep it from becoming emotionally closer. There is a tendency in this pattern to use it as a defense mechanism to keep your feelings hidden. You could be questioning the potential of a relationship too quickly without giving it a fair chance to develop. When this pattern grows too dominant, your relationship world lacks hope of finding fulfillment.

Lack of Imagination

This pattern indicates you are too locked into a grounded way of viewing the world. You can get into a predictable routine that works for you but not necessarily for someone else. When this occurs, you could be rejecting the dreams of someone you care about. Your own idealism and intuition might be too tied down to an overused left-brain approach. If this pattern becomes too dominant, it may keep you from supporting the ideas that are outside of your normal way of thinking. A lack of flexibility gets in the way of lessening the impact of this past-life influence. When you are not willing to reach out to the passionate ideas of others in their way of expressing an alternative perspective, this past-life pattern remains too strong.

Scapegoating

This past-life energy becomes a shadow force when you want to blame someone else for your problems. It works as a defense mechanism to keep you from taking responsibility for actions that offend people. You will not get the cooperation you need to reach a mutual agreement on important decisions that impact you and people you need on your team. The harmony you long to attain will remain out of reach when you surrender to the impulse to make use of the negative energy embedded in this pattern. Stubborn resistance to admitting you are wrong becomes a regular behavior. This might be due to a need to be perceived by others as being right. Hiding inner feelings of insecurity is another way this pattern emerges.

This is a past-life pattern that could get introduced through a person you know. The universe is giving you a preview of a behavior you once displayed in some past lives that you came into this incarnation to transcend. Rather than embodying this shadowy influence from your own past, you have been given an opportunity to first recognize it in another individual. You can choose not to walk down this same path again.

One Is the Loneliest Number

It is okay if you have decided living alone works for you. But what if a life of solitude is not your first choice? It is very possible a past-life energy is coming between you and settling comfortably into a relationship. The closer someone tries to come to you, the more you tend to pull away. A type of closeness-and-distance seesaw becomes all too present in your intimate relationships. A lack of trust is at the root of this pattern. Your emotional world is carefully protected to the point of keeping others locked out. Sharing your inner world with someone feels like crossing a vast ocean. Letting someone know you need them is difficult.

Altered Perceptions: Capricorn Paths to Transforming Karmic Relationship Patterns

It is a magical journey to explore ways to overcome past-life patterns. As you begin the path to new self-discovery, it does take some effort, along with great patience. If you identify with any of the past-life patterns discussed, chances are they have carried over from more than one past life. The good news is if you overcome this past-life shadow during this incarnation, it balances out all those past-life memories into a positive force.

It might seem like your eyes have a new vision as you awaken to the hold of a past-life pattern. Don't be discouraged if you feel like you have taken a step backward in overcoming past-life energies. This is a normal part of the process. There will come a time you will find the inner strength to rise above the hold of a karmic pattern. You will appreciate the renewed sense of personal power. You will enjoy a greater harmony in all your personal relationships. Letting go of the hold of a past-life pattern widens the road to finding more fulfillment in your relationships. That first acknowledgment of a past-life pattern is the key to opening up a more productive channeling of what was once a negative expression into new positive insights.

I Am the Boss

This pattern only needs you to understand you don't always have to be in control in your relationships. Allowing room for a loved one to declare their own territory encourages greater trust working for each of you. A partner or friend declaring their own independence actually takes much less of your energy than them looking for your approval of their decisions. The bells of harmony ring much louder when you move away from this past-life influence. Each time you consciously attempt to let others express their opinions freely, it becomes an automatic way of interacting with people. It is in surrendering the impulse to be bossy that the individuals you want to influence become attracted to your needs.

Rigid Focus

The rigid focus pattern only needs you to take that Capricorn power of concentration you possess and not forget to pay attention to those around you. You can train yourself to listen to the ideas of those you care about. It often makes a plan of action better if you include the insights of individuals you trust. You only need to slow down that powerful focusing talent you can display and make others feel their own goals are valued. Flexibility is the key to unlocking the hold of this past-life shadow energy. Your mind is energized and gains support from others when you show you can adapt to change. Your relationships increase in love and happiness when you walk away from this past-life pattern.

On My Guard

The on my guard pattern is asking you to stop overprotecting your feelings if you want to experience love and intimacy on a deeper level. When you reveal some of your emotional nature, you stimulate closeness and trust. You don't need to share all your secrets, but letting someone experience you beyond only the mental level forms a stronger lasting bond. It takes time to truly get to know someone in a relationship. Letting someone into your inner world speeds up the process of feeling like you are in a promising relationship. Showing vulnerability is not a sign of weakness but rather a show of attractive strength.

Conditional Love

The conditional love pattern is easier to overcome if you loosen up your approach to expressing love for others. You don't need to be setting rules when it comes to showing your warmth toward someone. You will soon realize your relationships are more enjoyable when you are not making up conditions. Romantic love has a power of its own. The universe has a magical way of giving you pleasant surprises when you don't worry about trying to control outcomes. You are going to receive much more emotional support and love when surrendering conditions imposed on others. This past-life influence will be less of a problem when you understand love cannot be conditional. When you trust someone, there is great joy to be experienced in the shared journey.

Addicted to Negative Thinking

Buddha said, "Be vigilant; guard your mind against negative thoughts."[1]
The addicted to negative thinking pattern needs you to think in a new,
invigorated positive direction. Negativity drains energy, whereas putting your mind in a positive framework enhances your ability to refrain
from judging others as well as yourself. It is true this past-life shadow
can be linked to being too guided by perfection. It is a trap to get
negative because someone is not perfect enough. If you channel that
wonderful Capricorn focus into a positive mindset, your relationships
become empowered. Better yet, those special people you care about
join forces with you in a harmony that cannot be denied.

There is a possibility you could come face-to-face with this pattern through someone else carrying it. Think of it as an opportunity
to not walk down the same path as a person you encounter. If you
maintain traveling in the positive lane, there is less of an opportunity for this pattern of thinking to infiltrate your perceptions. Each
of us will entertain negative thoughts at times. There is less likelihood you will fall back into repeating this past-life pattern if you
practice putting your positive instincts to the forefront.

Weak Assertiveness

The weak assertiveness pattern will need you to take a chance to
once in a while throw caution to the wind and boldly make your
insights known. It may take some practice if this does not come
naturally. You are more likely to enjoy witnessing yourself coming
out from behind the curtain and assertively making sure your voice
is heard. Your relationships get more in balance when people get a
chance to experience your true opinions. When you rise above this

---

1. Ecknath Easwaran, *Essence of the Dhammapada: The Buddha's Call to Nirvana*
   (Tomales, CA: Nilgiri Press, 2013), 266.

past-life influence, there is a better chance you will attract partners who have a mutual willingness to listen to your input about major decisions. The leadership instincts in Capricorn come alive when you take that leap of faith to speak from your heart. The fear of revealing your true needs to someone will lessen when you walk out of the shadows of this past-life pattern.

Too Austere

This pattern is converted from a limiting energy into a more expansive one with a new flexible attitude. You don't need to compromise your own values but do need to create enough space in a relationship for someone to feel mutually accepted. Trading in a narrow set of expectations for an openness to another person's need for independence helps a relationship grow. There is an inner sense of knowing boundaries in Capricorn. When you are not infringing on someone else's territory, the harmony becomes a reality. Relinquishing a tendency to hold on to a predetermined agenda allows the universe to deliver a package in a relationship far greater than you imagined.

Workaholic

The workaholic pattern comes down to finding a balance between work and making a commitment of time to those you love. If you make this a continuing plan there is a great chance your relationships stay on even keel. If you are making sure you listen to the people you care about and support their own needs, the happiness you desire will occur. Capricorn gives you an extra dose of devotion to a job. You only need to turn some of that focus to quality time with your special people. You have a great capacity to compartmentalize work and time with a loved one.

Remember to work harder on a problem than a person. You will bring someone closer if you let them be themselves. The shared independence in your relationships is what makes being together a true treasure of wealth.

Sad Outlook

The sad outlook pattern needs you to look for the best qualities in others rather than concentrating on their shortcomings. Each of us has areas where there is room for improvement. It is more likely you will find harmony in a relationship when you maintain a positive attitude. It will keep you from falling back into this past-life influence. If you do find yourself starting to display this pattern, again, don't panic. It will take some practice to walk in a new direction. Rather than leaving a relationship too fast, try giving it a fair chance to evolve. If you take the risk of revealing your deeper feelings, you might begin to perceive you have found someone with whom to share a wealth of happiness. Opening up to a more positive outlook is the real key to rising above the clouds of this pattern to new, brighter, happier skies.

Lack of Imagination

The lack of imagination pattern will not become a repeating past-life influence if you open your mind to listening to the hopes and dreams of others. Capricorn gives you a pragmatic and logical mind. When you step out of a too-grounded mental framework, you let your intuition into the inner world of those you love. You don't have to walk along the same footsteps of someone close to you, but you do need to accept their own belief system. Supporting the goal of a person you care about, even if it is somewhat out of your normal thinking, brings that person to support your own plans. If you show flexibility, it creates a bridge between you and someone you love that promises fulfillment and a long-lasting trust.

Scapegoating

The scapegoating pattern can be kept from occurring once again in the current incarnation through taking responsibility for your actions. If you refrain from blaming others when life is not going how you want it to be, this past-life influence stays away. Finding the humility to admit a mistake is the sure way to keeping peace and harmony in your relationships. Capricorn can provide you with a persona that projects outer strength. If you come out from behind the mask and show your vulnerability, people find it easier to trust you.

If it is true that a person close to you is exhibiting this pattern of behavior, consider it your chance to recognize you don't need to make this thinking part of your own life path. You could have come into this lifetime to shed this past-life pattern from your own reality. It is an opportunity to heal this past-life memory.

One Is the Loneliest Number

This pattern becomes a less lonely life if you are willing to take the risk of trusting someone in an intimate relationship. It may take an act of courage to let your guard down. It is very possible that in some past lives, rejection really hurt. You came here to shake off the influence of this past-life shadow. It would only take one very positive experience with a person to send this past-life memory packing. There can be caution in Capricorn to release a fear of failure. You may find it easier than you think to open up to a new perspective about relationships. Taking small steps to letting someone into your life will become a bigger path to experiencing joy. Let your intuition guide you forward so the universe can make it possible to find relationship fulfillment.

The Capricorn Reward from Solving Karmic Patterns

There is a tenacity in the sign Capricorn to solve a problem and not give up until the job is finished. That same determination gives you the edge in mastering the challenge presented by any past-life pattern. There is the possibility your mind might tell you the progress you hoped to make has stalled. If you keep trying to make a conscious effort, eventually you will see how far you have really come. In some ways it is like climbing a mountain. The view from the top makes the journey worth the effort.

If one or more of the karmic patterns seemed like part of your reality, don't let it worry you. Each of us has brought past-life patterns to work on into this incarnation. The main thing is having the awareness to grow. Patience in trying to heal a past-life pattern is good to remember. It does not matter how many past lives you may have repeated a past pattern in. If you resolve it in this lifetime, you put all those past lives in balance.

Maintaining a positive attitude helps overcome a karmic pattern and steer you toward relationship harmony. The possibilities to enjoy love and peace in relating to others increases greatly when you gain insight into a past-life shadow. Your insights will feel like they have clearer vision and attracting happiness with others will become your new reality.

ELEVEN

AQUARIUS: THE INDIVIDUALIST

Dates: January 20 to February 18

Element: Air

Strengths: Inventive, independent, trendsetting

Challenges: Too unpredictable, aloof, listening to opposing viewpoints

Karmic Relationship Primary Shadow: Resisting change

Key to Transforming Karmic Patterns: Listening to intuition

The Aquarius Current-Life Relationship Landscape

If you were born under the sign of Aquarius, your relationships often begin in surprising ways. You lean toward the unconventional but can enter relationships with individuals whose values differ from your own. It is that unpredictable side of you that some people find attractive, but there are others who are not interested. The traditional astrology phrase for Aquarius is "I invent." You do have a tendency to have a wide variety of social contacts. There is that inner drive to find a soul mate to mutually share your life adventures.

Your mind likely works fast. People who don't expect you to make decisions faster than you prefer to are appreciated. There is a stubborn resistance to change that is not on your own terms.

You may hold back your feelings until you really trust someone. Your intellect can hold back emotions like a strong dam. That intuitive side of you stays clear if your relationships don't worry you. Independent individuals excite you. They stimulate your creative imagination. You enjoy someone who supports your goals and does not depend on you too heavily too much of the time.

You can grow impatient with people who seem to be holding back the truth from you. Some will not perceive your emotional sensitivity right away. Your thought-provoking mind might conceal your feelings.

Anger at times makes you nervous. You prefer rational individuals who like to solve problems logically. If there is an angry disagreement, you want it to be over quickly. You likely don't want to waste time disagreeing about small details.

Your freedom is a big deal. Having your space to reflect and process is a major need. You like people who are not afraid to pursue a dream and will not interfere with your own.

The Aquarius Past-Life Karmic Relationship Patterns

Don't be disturbed if you identify with any of the past-life patterns that will be discussed. Think of this as a learning experience. Everyone has issues that can surface once again from past lifetimes. Those memories are residing in our consciousness. The main thing to remember is that the information in this book is there to empower you and open up paths to greater relationship fulfillment. Your first steps to look for more ways to express energies through new insights might become awakened.

As an Aquarius, you may be able to use your mental determination to break new ground regarding any past-life pattern. It does take practice and patience when trying to change a behavior. If you hold on to that forward vision you possess, it could surprise you how fast you can turn a negative past-life theme into a positive. That desire to attract the right people and abundance into your life is closer than you may think.

Different Just to Be Different

If this past-life pattern followed you into this incarnation, it is expressed as purposely taking the opposite point of view. There is a self-orientation to get your own way. There is little thought of trying to really reach a mutual understanding. The root of this past-life influence could be hidden anger. Rather than communicating directly about what you need, you have an urge to be contradictory. This pattern does not serve you well in having a close relationship based on trust. You are not listening to someone to truly understand their own needs.

Escape into the Future

If activated, this past-life pattern finds you not wanting to deal with issues in the present. Your mind is so much on the future that a lover or friend might wonder if they can count on you when a situation calls for this. Aquarius is a goal-oriented sign. It is only when those future plans get you to ignore the goals of someone close to you that there is a problem. Others could perceive you as irresponsible, while you see this as an eagerness to pursue your dreams. If you fail to let others in on your restless search for the promise of tomorrow, it causes confusion. The underlying cause of this pattern may be linked to a fear of adversity. Rather than deal with the daily routines, you prefer the excitement of the future that is constantly calling to you. This pattern can be linked to running away from conflict when it arises in a relationship. The hope is that a problem will disappear if you don't face it, which can make an issue grow worse between you and another person.

Life in the Fast Lane

Your sign is one of the faster-moving mental signs. It can be a challenge for people to stay on the same page with you when you suddenly want to change directions. It is when you stay unpredictable that this past-life pattern grows in intensity. Stability in a relationship could be difficult to attain. The adrenaline rush of constantly wanting to start new endeavors can create turmoil with those you love. Living for the excitement outweighs wanting to be in a committed relationship. Not paying enough attention to the needs of others causes them to hold back from supporting your goals.

I Think, Therefore I Am

The mental processes come so automatically to an Aquarius that it is like being in cruise control while driving. Crossing over into the emotional lane is difficult when this pattern emerges. If you are reluctant to express any feelings, people closest to you may perceive you as uncaring. This pattern can be well hidden from your conscious memory. It might come as a surprise if someone lets you know that your emotional communication is lacking. This pattern can be a defense mechanism to conceal your inner world from others. It does create a challenge to give others a read on how you really feel about situations that arise.

It is possible this pattern makes an appearance through a person you have met. They don't ever seem comfortable in talking on the emotional level. It may be that you have managed to steer clear of this past-life shadow in this incarnation. You just need to maintain your clarity and not get pulled into it.

Derailing the Goals of Others

A signal this past-life pattern has become a player in your life is if you negate the goals of others too much of the time. There is a tendency to show a lack of faith in individuals needing your positive support. People can feel discounted when you are not getting behind their plans. A resentment starts to unfold, causing others not to give you the support you need. If it becomes a regular occurrence, this pattern alienates the very people you hope to remain close to. Sometimes this past-life shadow will show itself if you are uncomfortable with a relationship partner wanting to come closer. This is your way of distancing yourself.

Don't Crowd Me

There is an instinctual need for freedom built into the sign Aquarius. If you get too set on having space in a moment's notice, it can catch those trying to get close to you off guard. The need to roam freely with no boundaries can be a big ask of your lovers and friends. Some people may perceive you as aloof, while you feel this is you being yourself. If you are unreasonable in your need for space, you are going to be seen as pushing people away. A failure to communicate the need for great breathing room clearly causes confusion in your relationships. You could be looked at as too invisible when someone needs you. A commitment is difficult to maintain if you choose to live like an individual with little awareness that you truly want to create a sense of togetherness.

Lost in a Cause

There can be a tendency to feel a great allegiance to a group with a shared cause. This pattern can manifest if you are so dedicated to influences outside of your relationship that you ignore a partner. This could be a past-life tendency that you are repeating. A lover or soul mate will begin to resent the time taken away from the relationship if you seem missing in action. It is when you treat a group or cause as your lover that it can create a sense of separation in a relationship. It can put great stress on a relationship when there is a lack of balance in juggling what you feel you need from pursuing a cause with what you need from a lover. It isn't that you can't live in both worlds. It is that it does not work when someone close to you feels left out of a big chunk of your life. People who love you want to know you will make time for them. They want to know you need them.

Not Learning from the Past

Having your mind on tomorrow more than today is sometimes part of the normal Aquarius business-as-usual thinking. This past-life influence could find you bored with the present. Dealing with everyday life can seem bothersome. There may be an attitude that issues in a relationship disappear if you escape into dreaming about future plans. You could keep repeating behaviors over and over that cause friction with others no matter how much they point this out. A stubborn refusal to compromise causes a great lack of cooperation from others. This past-life shadow is keeping you from learning from past mistakes made in relationships in this life and from past incarnations. It is less obvious that some behaviors being repeated in the current incarnation are from past lives. These shadows living in our memory are not easy to identify. They can suddenly appear as if they have a life of their own.

Extreme Impatience

A signal this past-life pattern could be too much a part of your self-expression is thinking everyone in your life moves too slowly. To many, your brain could seem like a fast-moving taxi driver in a large city changing lanes in a hurry. It does cause tension in your relationships if you show impatience on a regular basis. It will appear to others that your own way of getting things done is more important than their way. This usually results in arguments and hurt feelings. Being born as an Aquarius does indicate your mind has the potential to be three steps out in front of other people. When you don't slow down enough, you can end up losing individuals you need in your life.

It is possible this pattern can show up in your life through a person you have grown close to. It is an opportunity to get a glimpse of this past-life shadow in someone else. The key thing is not to walk down this path yourself.

Fear of Change

If this past-life pattern awakens, your resistance to change can disrupt the flow in your relationships. Being glued to fixed positions can alienate the people you are trying to keep close. Aquarius can be one of those astrological signs that want to have things on their own terms. If you latch on too tightly to this type of thinking, it can be difficult to adjust to changes in a relationship a partner might perceive as needed. This past-life theme often slips into the current incarnation when you don't trust the motives of another person. Or it can simply be that you want to remain in what you think are your own comfort zones. Being able to let yourself reach a mutual agreement with someone is a real challenge. You could be expecting others to do all the compromising, which usually puts a great deal of distance between you and a person with whom you hope to have a feeling of harmony.

Loss of Independence

When entering your current incarnation, this past-life pattern could show you attracting strong-minded individuals who overshadow your feelings of thinking for yourself. This runs contrary to that independent streak that travels through the mind of an Aquarius. Your own goals in this type of relationship often get put on hold to meet the needs of others. Your natural drive to find equality in a relationship is stalled if you are too compromising. Emotional confusion usually results if you stay locked into this past-life influence. Your assertiveness becomes too watered down from tiptoeing around those you are trying too hard to please. That equality you require to express your true voice is drowned out by someone not considering your own life pursuits.

Too Close for Comfort

If this past-life pattern becomes active, you find the greater the distance with a lover, the better off you feel. It can be a carryover from past lives in which a fear of abandonment was an issue. It makes it a challenge to open up emotionally if you find closeness makes you extremely uncomfortable. Most Aquarians prefer enough space in a relationship to feel like they can be themselves. The problem this past-life shadow presents is that it feels like there is never enough space to make you feel at ease with someone. Another way this past-life theme appears is through an anxious fear of a relationship ending with hurtful feelings. Your unwillingness to talk with a lover about your anxiety that the relationship will not be a success may keep this past-life theme a problem.

Altered Perceptions: Aquarius Paths to Transforming Karmic Relationship Patterns

There will be a great sense of relief when you work your way through a past-life pattern. The effort you make pays great dividends. Your mind will feel a new inspiration to express the knowledge gained in bringing a past-life shadow out into the light. Your relationships offer greater fulfillment when you make a bold statement in facing a past-life karmic influence. Courageously rising above the fog presented by a past-life pattern puts you on the road to relationship harmony.

Remember it takes patience and practice to navigate through these past-life memories that are still with you in this incarnation. There is no need to judge yourself if you feel a connection to any of these past-life patterns. Think of it as a learning experience along a journey of self-discovery. Don't be surprised if you take one step forward and two backward. It is an evolutionary process that, as you travel along, will reveal exciting new clarity. With each new insight your confidence will grow. Each of us has lessons to learn in the current life. You will realize as you gain increasing awareness of a pattern that it becomes easier to not let it come between you and those you love.

Different Just to Be Different

This pattern can be resolved by thinking in terms of win-win solutions. If you realize that your uniqueness is what people often are attracted to, there is no need to go to extremes. You will find that the closeness you hope to create with someone flows smoothly when you show you value the insights of others. You don't have to always agree with someone expressing their own perspective. If you are making an attempt to listen to others, it is a positive step to greater harmony in your relationships. Aquarius gives you a natural rebellious and freedom streak. Nobody can really take this away from you. Sharing your knowledge with others stimulates them to trust you, and their willingness to give you the space you need is more likely to occur.

Escape into the Future

The escape into the future pattern is lessened in its intensity when you balance what is expected of you in the present with the call of the future. Your Sun sign Aquarius will regularly get you to look forward with putting a plan into motion. If you can remember to communicate clearly with those who want to be included in your everyday life, this past-life pattern will not be a problem. Dealing with issues as they occur actually frees you to put your energy into your favorite pastimes. Facing adversity with a lover deepens the trust in the relationship. You may be surprised to learn that a problem is not as big as it seemed when you talk it through with someone. Taking the time to share ideas when tackling an issue is a way to achieve a feeling of togetherness.

Life in the Fast Lane

The life in the fast lane pattern is easier to handle when you don't get in too big of a hurry on a regular basis. It is easy to think everyone else has a speedy mind that doesn't need a lot of time to process life experiences. There is a side of Aquarius you can go to when needed that can find a slower rhythm. You can show a great ability to focus on the goals that you highly value. When you let others in on your thought processes, you don't shock them with sudden surprise. You do possess sharp communication skills. Intimacy and trust build as a foundation in your relationships when you pay attention to what people need from you. Sometimes it is pausing just long enough to notice the little things that make someone happy that brings them traveling in a lane of joy right alongside you.

I Think, Therefore I Am

This pattern only needs for you to come out from a well-defined mental fortress and show your feelings. People find you easier to understand when you show your emotions. Revealing your inner world might take some time, but when you do so, a lover can experience you on a deeper level. Your mental nature likes to connect with a person through words and concepts. This makes a great way to enter a relationship. But as a relationship progresses and you find the courage to express your feelings, you will open the door to experience greater closeness with someone.

This pattern may have come into your life expressed through a person you are involved with in a relationship. Try to realize this is an opportunity to get a view of this pattern and an opportunity to not accept this past-life shadow into your own reality.

Derailing the Goals of Others

The derailing the goals of others pattern is turned around quickly by dropping a negative attitude when someone needs positive support from you. The chances of creating a harmonious relationship increase greatly when you show you care about the success of a loved one's plan. The flow of love and an equal exchange of positive encouragement for goals is enhanced with less criticism. You don't have to agree on everything. But you will find your relationships are more fulfilling when you offer helpful insights to those needing it from you. When you show you are paying attention and honoring the dreams of someone, chances are they want to remain close to you. This past-life shadow that has followed you into this incarnation is not going to get activated when you offer your most loving support to a person you care about.

Don't Crowd Me

This pattern is less problematic if you understand you need to communicate your freedom needs clearly. Generally speaking, Aquarians like yourself appreciate much breathing room in relationships. If you act responsibly and really participate actively with a lover, you likely will be granted the freedom you require. The main thing to remember is that the important people in your life want to know you will be there when needed. A key way to keep this past-life pattern very dormant is to have some shared activities with people you love and want to be close to. It is a sure way to get the private time you need. There is a good chance a partner will appreciate some alone time for themselves. Time to yourself is not a problem when people in your life know they are never far from your thoughts and heart.

Lost in a Cause

The lost in a cause pattern lessens in its influence when you show enough flexibility by not dedicating all of yourself to a group or cause. It is okay if it stimulates your mind to connect with a group. It is important to keep this pattern from playing the trickster and occupying too much of your time and to not ignore the people you depend on in your life. It is essential to consciously allot time to a relationship to keep it growing. Being an Aquarius, you can have great focus when you feel passionate about a cause. The key thing to remember is to not let pursuing a group identity or a cause become more important than the love you feel for someone. Making a genuine effort to spend quality time with a special person is a clear way to rise above this past-life pattern.

Not Learning from the Past

This pattern is easier to manage when you make a concentrated effort to deal with present issues in a relationship. Your mind will always to some degree think about what steps to take to accomplish future goals. When you show you are remembering not to repeat behaviors that anger others, this pattern fades far into the background. Being willing to adapt to change in a relationship is a sure way to send this pattern out of your life. The past is a great teacher when we learn not to repeat actions that disrupt the peace in a relationship. There are new insights that can be gained in accepting the reality that working in a spirit of cooperation with those you love is the path to great harmony.

Extreme Impatience

The extreme impatience pattern is easier to resolve if you take the time to get some input from a partner or close friend before speeding ahead on an idea. Getting some insight from someone else to compare to your own is one way to let a person know you value their opinion. Chances are people know in the end you will make your own independent choices. Paying attention to an individual close to you is just like magic in conquering this past-life pattern. It then does not really matter if you happen to be one of those fast-thinking and quick-to-act Aquarians. There is an objective and reflective dimension to Aquarius that comes into play when you slow down. It never hurts to pause and consider how your fast pace is impacting those around you. When you include the special people in your life in a plan, you are more apt to get the support and encouragement you would love to have. Past-life shadow energies residing in our memory are less likely to surface in your current incarnation when you focus on creating harmony rather than discord.

If this pattern is coming at you through someone else in your life, it is the universe giving you a preview of the impact of this behavior. Consider it an opportunity to be a watcher of this pattern rather than a player in it. It could be a karmic pattern you came into this life not to engage in once again.

Fear of Change

The fear of change pattern is one in which you are challenged to be more flexible. When you are able to do so, life with others has a flowing atmosphere. Intimacy comes naturally, and the love given and received is a great feeling. Letting go of very fixed ways of doing things makes it easier to dance with the minds of others in a shared rhythm. When you step out of your own comfort zones now and then, it is easier to walk into the comfort zones of others and enjoy the experience. It is more likely someone will then be more accepting of your own likes and dislikes. Trust between you and people you want to establish closeness with comes easier when you show a willingness to be open to new ideas.

Loss of Independence

The loss of independence pattern is overcome by not fearing the need to walk to your own drumbeat. Those initial quiet steps to being more assertive will eventually be followed by louder ones. A feeling of independence is the oxygen an Aquarian must experience to feel confident. Staying clear of those people who are too controlling may be needed. You thrive on relationships that are based on equality. When you don't do all the compromising, it strengthens you mentally and emotionally. Your natural instincts are to desire an equal give-and-take in relationships. Your goals in life feel empowered when you are in a partnership with someone you trust. It is then you fly free like an eagle and this past-life pattern is no longer an influence in the current life.

Too Close for Comfort

The too close for comfort pattern needs you to take the risk of trusting someone enough to come closer. Usually the fear of something is worse than the actual experience. This past-life influence will lessen in its interference when you communicate honestly with someone. Aquarius is a strong mental sign. If you allow your emotions to get expressed, closeness grows more comfortable. It takes retraining your mind to allow feelings to come through you to a lover. Trust often really is the key to overcoming this pattern. You need to believe that you are strong enough to sustain a relationship and you can allow a person to get to know you on a deeper level. Don't worry if this feels awkward at first. It will take some practice.

The effort will pay off as it creates a bridge to greater intimacy and harmony.

The Aquarius Reward from Solving Karmic Patterns

The long-range vision of Aquarius is hard to match by any other astrological sign. The ruling planet of Aquarius is Uranus. This planet orbits in a unique way sitting on its side, while all the other planets orbit in a straight up and down movement. Likewise, the sign Aquarius can display a laser-like insight in rising above any karmic pattern. It will take steady focus and consistent effort to outlast the influence of a past-life shadow. Each step along the journey does produce more confidence as you gain a foothold in walking away from past-life patterns that have possibly interfered with your relationship happiness.

The Rolling Stones song "Get Off of My Cloud" is sometimes how you may feel in wanting to walk to the sound of your own drumbeat. Your innate ability to break free from the hold of a past-life influence helps you gain a new sense of self-discovery.

Be patient as you gain greater awareness of any karmic pattern. Enjoy the growth and fulfillment that can come your way as you move into new insights. The reward for walking on the road that is often less traveled is being brought into the light of personal and relationship harmony.

TWELVE
PISCES: THE DREAMER

Dates: February 19 to March 20

Element: Water

Strengths: Intuitive power, being supportive, strong belief in oneself and others

Challenges: Not grounded, unrealistic expectations, confused dependency needs

Karmic Relationship Primary Shadow: Hiding from true insights

Key to transforming Karmic Patterns: Balancing dreams with reality

The Pisces Current-Life Relationship Landscape

If you were born under the sign Pisces, your mental and emotional energies like to ride alongside each other. The traditional astrology slogan for Pisces is "I believe." This implies you like to have dreams and ideals that inspire you. People who can accept this part of your identity are welcomed and those who don't have a more difficult time understanding you. It isn't that you are not reality oriented. Your ambition has to be fueled by passion and some degree of emotional award. Individuals loving you the way you are make it easier to form a close relationship with them.

Your closest lovers and friends might share your love of the arts. You are generous to those you feel deserving of your generosity. Individuals who lean on you too heavily for emotional or material support can be draining. Knowing your boundaries comes with experience. Guilt is something you have to overcome. You realize sooner or later you can't please everyone all the time.

Falling in love is a powerful spiritual experience for you. Searching for a soul mate is an innate desire. Knowing whom to trust is a learning process. Finding a person who seems to read you without speaking is not so uncommon. There are times people will ask you to speak your mind.

Meeting new friends or lovers might seem like a magical synchronicity created by the universe. You like individuals with a belief system that makes sense to you. Someone giving you confidence through believing in you captures your heart.

You don't have much use for people bringing unneeded stress into your life. Peace and quiet are preferred over exhausting arguments. Your privacy is sacred and must be respected. You don't want to be controlled by anyone but do want an intimacy you can trust. You have a natural feeling of compassion for those you care about. You will fight to protect your beliefs and what you love.

The Pisces Past-Life Karmic Relationship Patterns

If you connect with any of the past-life patterns that will be discussed, don't let it bother you. The idea is to gain greater awareness about past-life influences and to get a more positive expression in dealing with them. Each of us has brought in past-life shadow energies we are trying to bring out into the light of clarity. Think of it as an evolutionary journey. So remember there is no need to judge yourself. It is an evolving learning process.

As a Pisces, your faith in your ability to rise above a karmic pattern is within your reach at all times. The road to greater relationship harmony becomes clearer in acknowledging one of these patterns. It takes practice and patience, so don't get discouraged if you find yourself falling back into a past-life thought pattern. These memories from past incarnations can be healed in this lifetime. Don't worry about being too perfect. It can seem messy as you begin the path to transcending the hold of a past-life pattern. Just keep moving forward and before you know it, you will perceive your new growth. Self-discovery is exciting.

Don't Make Any Waves

This pattern makes itself known if you fear facing adversity in a relationship. There is a tendency to hide your displeasure with someone's actions, thinking it will maintain peace and quiet. The issues you have with someone don't go away. Pisces is a water sign that can find you wanting things to always flow smoothly with others. A failure to communicate what you need from a person does eventually lead to frustration for both of you. Enabling the behavior you find bothersome rather than calling it out causes anger to build. Your moods can suddenly swing to extremes as your emotional intensity builds in this pattern. Defining a relationship clearly becomes a major challenge.

Helpless Victim

Dependency needs get out of balance if this past-life pattern gets activated. You can find yourself having unrealistic expectations for emotional support. It does begin to drain the energy of others. If you are always needing to be saved from situations you have gotten into, it begins to put tremendous strain on a relationship. This pattern often is caused by a lack of clarity about what you want from a relationship. Not taking enough responsibility for important decisions that are needed in a relationship can result in frustration for each of you. You are relinquishing too much control to someone else. Your own sense of personal power is being too limited.

This past-life influence can show up through a lover constantly acting helpless to get attention. It might be a pattern you have come into this life to overcome that is getting revealed to you through a person you know intimately. It is your opportunity to perceive this pattern clearly before you embrace it for yourself.

Love Is Blind

You could be in a relationship in which your boundaries are very blurred. The idealism of Pisces is sometimes way out in front of the reality. In this past-life pattern you might be superimposing your imagination onto someone and perceiving that a partner can do no wrong. Falling in love is a powerful emotional experience. If this pattern gets activated from your past-life memory, you may have trouble being objective about someone. It is possible your own needs could become lost in trying to fulfill whatever a lover wants from you. When you enter relationships too fast without giving it some time to make sure a person is who they seem to be, this past-life shadow grows stronger.

Emotional Rescuer

A signal this past-life pattern has been activated is if you feel you must always fix the problems of others. Your sound reasoning gets lost in an emotional fog. You can't really save someone from having to deal with their problems. Your good intentions may be prolonging an issue for a person in that they keep repeating it. You probably become disappointed with someone doing the same behavior over and over again that you are trying to fix. This is offering emotional support but having expectations of yourself and others that are unreasonable. This pattern can become a bad habit if you think you must assume the responsibility for the problems created by others.

Looking for Perfection

There are no perfect people. But if you fall into this past-life pattern, your mind can become too attached to looking for a perfect partner. It puts much pressure on you and someone else to live up to unrealistic expectations. There will always be divine discontent embedded in this pattern, meaning you will keep finding flaws in a person. It makes forming a solid relationship next to impossible. This is accepting a self-imposed mission that is truly a tall mountain to complete. To stay on this path only results in disappointment.

This pattern you came into this life to gain clarity about could be presented through someone expecting too much perfection from you. This will sooner or later be realized as expectations you cannot fulfill. Think of this as the universe showing you a behavior you don't want to make part of your own thinking in this incarnation.

Cold Feet

If this past-life pattern becomes too much a player in your life, it is difficult to make a serious commitment to a relationship. You may have met someone who seems like the right partner for you. But as the person wants to get to know you on a deeper level, it causes you to pull back. It may puzzle you why this keeps occurring in your relationships. Embedded in your mind are past-life memories in which you could have had trouble with trust due to emotional pain. You can't seem to break through a hesitation to establish a long, stable relationship. If you are happy with living alone, this is no problem. But if you want to live with a lover in a committed relationship, this pattern is troublesome.

Running from Adversity

Pisces can be a supersensitive sign. You can feel the energy of people in a room more than they realize. It is this same tuning in to the feelings of others that can cause this past-life pattern to emerge. You anticipate the coming friction over an issue with someone, but your first impulse is to avoid dealing with the problem. Usually what you are choosing to escape from only enlarges your differences with people. The emotional distance between you and a lover becomes a vast ocean if you don't communicate more openly. Every relationship, no matter how wonderful, will have a bit of conflict. If not dealt with at some point, this past-life shadow can cause you to miss out on good relationships that have a promise of harmony.

Sounds of Silence

There are times when being quiet and reflective is good for the mind. Then there are instances when people need to hear what is in your thoughts. If this past-life pattern is too active in your life, you can become too withdrawn. If you become too invisible when your input is needed, the important people in your life will perceive this as an avoidance behavior. When you expect someone to read your mind, it can result in confusion. Others may think that your silence is a disapproval of their ideas or actions. Leaving too much up for interpretation by not communicating causes distance from those you want to bring closer. Pisces is a water sign that at times retreats to recharge the mental energies. It is the extreme absence of a vibrant presence in a relationship that reveals this pattern occupies too big a part of your thought processes.

Paradise Lost

If this past-life pattern becomes activated, you have a tendency to look for the negative in others without trying to notice the positive. It could be from a memory linked to some past lives from relationships that did not live up to your expectations. Your mental filters are too stuck on losing faith that you will find a person that makes you feel happy. There is a side of Pisces that is a true romantic. Falling in love may feel good to you. It is accepting the day-to-day living with someone that worries you. Life can get messy and issues do arise. If you remain fixed on the idea you can find a relationship without ever having to face some adversity, then this pattern becomes too much a part of your reality.

Coloring the Truth

This past-life influence finds you telling people what you think they want to hear. It may be twisting the truth to keep someone liking you. It may be a way of manipulating situations to get what you feel you need from a person. Your negotiations with individuals are more like business transactions than emotional. Trust is often lacking in this pattern. You don't really want to let anyone into your inner world. You are more comfortable staying on the mental level with others, masking your fear of a true emotional intimacy.

Overly residing in the walls of this past-life shadow prevents you from obtaining a deeper, fulfilling love.

Comparison Shopping

This past-life pattern could find you searching over and over again for a person who reminds you of a past-life lover. There is a good chance you are not aware you are doing this. It does present a challenge because finding someone who is the perfect replacement is impossible. Not letting go of the lover from the past makes it difficult to create enough room for a new person to enter your life. It is possible this pattern may become so dominantly connected to a past-life relationship that it is locked in your memory. It has you seeking someone who perfectly matches the qualities of that past-life lover. It will keep you frustrated due to looking for someone planted in your imagination who may never appear.

My Truth Is the Truth

You become too particular about how you like things done when this past-life pattern has gained too much strength. People will perceive you as too uncompromising. It might be that your mind has trouble considering alternatives to your own ideas. Inflexibility has a tendency to alienate the people you want to support your goals. Closeness turns quickly into distance if you rigidly hold on to your own opinions. Rather than operating as an open-minded team player, you could be putting on a solo act as others feel pushed away.

Altered Perceptions: Pisces Paths to Transforming Karmic Relationship Patterns

Overcoming a karmic pattern frees you in several ways. You can attain a more optimistic attitude about relationships. It can feel like a new vitality has occurred. What was once a shadow from a past life interfering with your relationship happiness has disappeared. The effort to move beyond the negative gravity of a past-life influence is well worth the effort. It is easier to attract the right people into your life by moving beyond a past-life energy.

If you identified with any of the karmic patterns that were discussed, try not to let it worry you. Each of us has brought some past-life experiences into the current incarnation that we are trying to gain insight into. Think of this as a path of self-discovery. The opportunity to explore an alternative way to express a past-life energy opens new doors to relationship harmony. Those first awakenings about past-life patterns can stimulate your mind into productive, life-changing perceptions. The growth along this journey can feel exciting. You will likely come to the realization that there is no turning back. The path forward will call to you to keep seeking greater understanding of any past-life pattern.

Don't Make Any Waves

This pattern is less of an echo in your mind if you take the first steps to be more assertive. People assume you don't mind their treatment of you if you fail to speak up. It could seem awkward at first to say what you have been holding back. With practice it does get easier. Your relationships stay in balance when you voice your opinions openly. Anger has less of a chance to build if you communicate your thoughts. Your insights get empowered as you let others hear them. Your mind, body, and spirit find their natural alignment as you verbalize your ideas. Harmony in your relationships resonates when you engage with others in lively discussions.

Helpless Victim

The helpless victim pattern requires you to get your dependency needs balanced. You don't need to take on all the responsibility for decisions in a relationship. You only need to focus on pulling your own weight. Think in terms of equality and you are most of the way there in overcoming this past-life shadow. Tuning in to your own personal power attracts the right types of people into your life to experience fulfillment. Paying attention to what others need makes it more likely they will do the same for you. Your relationships receive rays of harmony when you don't always lean too heavily on others for emotional support.

If you are in a relationship with a person who exhibits this pattern, consider it a preview of a behavior you came into this lifetime to reject. The universe is showing you a past-life influence you need to recognize but not embrace.

Love Is Blind

The influence of the love is blind pattern is lessened when you take the time to reality test relationships. Slow down and make sure what your imagination is telling you about a person is real. You need to define your boundaries clearly. Pisces emotions grow strong when falling in love. There is nothing wrong with this. Just make sure you keep your objectivity tuned up because it helps keep your eyes open in a clearer way. Love and logic don't seem like they belong together when it comes to romance. But they are both needed to keep this past-life influence from manifesting in this incarnation.

Emotional Rescuer

The emotional rescuer pattern is less likely to trouble you when you learn to step back from always coming to the rescue for others.

It is better not to enable someone to keep getting into the same problems over and over again by thinking you are required to make everything right. It empowers you and those you care about to let them deal with their issues. You can be a supportive friend and lover without trying to assume all the responsibility. It is a needed learning experience to let someone face their challenges and even gain wisdom from mistakes. It is exhausting to think you must be the rescuer. Your own mental strength gets less drained when overcoming this past-life tendency. The big payoff is that your relationships will become more enjoyable and fulfilling.

Looking for Perfection

The looking for perfection pattern is easier to navigate if you set more realistic expectations. The harder you try to change someone into an image that resembles perfection in your mind, the more that person is likely to resist changing just to please you. If you accept a flexible attitude, you will be happier. Letting go of trying to control or manipulate a person to fit into an idealized portrait of what you think they should be is a better path. Creating a relationship together with someone yields a much better composite or sense of unity. There is always some compromise in every successful partnership, whether a business or a romantic one. The universe has a better chance to give you a harmonious relationship when you put away the perfect script in favor of a magical, surprising one.

There is a chance you can encounter a person who portrays this pattern that you came into this life to overcome. This would be your opportunity to perceive this behavior as something you don't want to accept as part of your own reality.

Cold Feet

Pisces in astrology rules the feet. You don't need to have cold ones when it comes to the cold feet pattern. Taking the risk of letting someone get to know you on an emotional level does allow a deeper intimacy to form. You don't need to move too fast into a new relationship. Give it time to develop is one way to take the fear out of closeness. You need to convince yourself you have much to offer in a relationship. Look at the relationship experience as a journey. It usually takes time for the depth to reveal itself. If you never take a chance on someone, you will never know if you have found the right partner. Chances are someone you meet has their own fears. The key thing to remember in shaking loose from this past-life pattern is to trust yourself. The fear is usually worse than getting to know someone and learning how to have an enjoyable shared experience of each other.

Running from Adversity

The running from adversity pattern can be turned around by realizing your sensitive intuition, which senses trouble with someone ahead of time, only needs to be channeled toward thinking in terms of solutions. It takes less energy to confront a problem if someone is willing to work with you on solving it. Running away is not the same as taking a pause to gather your thoughts. Your relationships get empowered when you team up with a partner to deal with an issue. The more you practice doing this, the less likely this past-life shadow shows its face. You are stronger than you might realize. As you learn to engage assertively in handling challenges as they arise, this past-life pattern stays away.

Sounds of Silence

The sounds of silence pattern indicates a quietness that comes naturally to Pisces more than to many of the other astrological signs. Taking the initiative to speak up and be present when requested by others prevents this pattern from occurring. It is fine to need time alone to gather your thoughts and recharge your brain. Finding that balance between visibility and taking time alone keeps this past-life shadow force from making an entrance into this lifetime. It might take a conscious effort to realize you need to communicate your ideas. This pattern may not be so obvious to your conscious mind in your everyday interactions with people. With practice it will be an automatic response to be an active partner in a relationship. It builds trust when you show you are listening by speaking your thoughts openly to someone.

Paradise Lost

The paradise lost pattern is easier to let go of when you focus more on being positive. It is the sure road to finding harmony with someone. Learning to live with the ups and downs in a relationship is accepting the reality there are no perfect people. Supporting the goals of individuals you care about sends this pattern away from you. Being a cheerleader brings out the best in others. This does not mean you will like everything about someone. But the happiness you long for with a lover has a much better chance to occur when you perceive a person's good attributes. The bridge to attracting fulfillment in a relationship is truly believing in a person. Your positive support for others shows you appreciate them and want to keep them close.

Coloring the Truth

You can liberate yourself from the coloring the truth pattern when you communicate with an honest representation of yourself. Instead of trying to manipulate situations, you will find it less stressful to work toward win-win results with people. The big payoff is you can have a relationship based on trust. The love you want to receive is readily available when you stay away from only telling people what you imagine they want to hear. Letting someone into your feelings opens the door to a harmonious intimacy. It takes much less energy to be open about true perceptions rather than trying to conceal them. This past-life tendency is less problematic when you show you are bringing your most authentic game into a relationship.

Comparison Shopping

The influence of the comparison shopping pattern can be lessened if you come to grips with the reality that the past does not need to rule the present. Learning what you liked and learned from a past-life relationship is valuable. But it is important to remember it is time to allow someone new to come into your life. There is an excellent possibility that meeting someone new will bring a better match for the person you have evolved into in the current life. You could be in denial about what was not so good in a past-life relationship, only longing for what you liked about a person. Setting yourself free to explore the harmony you can create with a new love can liberate you from this past-life shadow.

My Truth Is the Truth

This pattern needs you to not lose sight that the opinions and ideas of others matter. Everyone wants to feel valued. Think in terms of inclusion and this past-life nemesis will stay away. It is easy for emotions to tell your mind that you have the best possible solution to a problem. Let the wonderful adaptability of your sign Pisces remind you that listening to input from people you love is great wisdom. You probably will need to slow down long enough to listen to your closest allies before running with a plan. Remember, there are many paths to the truth even though you could be convinced your own thoughts are the best. Stay away from being critical of those who try to support your goals with their own insights. The love and harmony you cherish stays strong when you open your mind to new ideas from those you trust.

The Pisces Reward from Solving Karmic Patterns

You are fortunate to be born a Pisces with a strong intuition. It gives you the capacity to believe that you can find your way to rise above the challenge presented by any karmic pattern. It takes determination and patience to face a past-life pattern. The first awareness of a past-life shadow is the beginning of a magical journey to self-discovery. Your emotions as a water sign are likely intense at times. When you step back and don't judge yourself, the insights into healing a past-life energy are very possible.

If you did see yourself in any of the past-life patterns discussed, don't let it make you feel overly anxious. Remember, this is a learning experience without a deadline to meet. Go at your own pace. If you feel like you are taking one step forward and then are backtracking, that is okay. The main thing is to keep moving forward on your evolving journey.

There is a big payoff in dealing with a past-life influence. Your relationships are easier to enjoy. Your way of relating gains a greater flow of harmony. The love you came into this life for unfolds in ways you may never have imagined. You will be better equipped to give more generously and to receive with an open heart.

To Write to the Author

If you wish to contact the author or would like more information about this book, please write to the author in care of Llewellyn Worldwide Ltd. and we will forward your request. Both the author and the publisher appreciate hearing from you and learning of your enjoyment of this book and how it has helped you. Llewellyn Worldwide Ltd. cannot guarantee that every letter written to the author can be answered, but all will be forwarded. Please write to:

Bernie Ashman
℅ Llewellyn Worldwide
2143 Wooddale Drive
Woodbury, MN 55125-2989

Please enclose a self-addressed stamped envelope for reply,
or $1.00 to cover costs. If outside the U.S.A., enclose
an international postal reply coupon.

Many of Llewellyn's authors have websites with additional information and resources. For more information, please visit our website at http://www.llewellyn.com.